HOW TO BE HEARD

Ten Lessons Teachers Need to Advocate for Their Students and Profession

Celine Coggins

Foreword by John King

JB JOSSEY-BASS™
A Wiley Brand

Published by Jossey-Bass
A Wiley Brand

One Montgomery Street, Suite 1000, San Francisco, CA 94104-4594—www.josseybass.com

Jossey-Bass books and products are available through most bookstores. To contact Jossey-Bass directly call our Customer Care Department within the U.S. at 800-956-7739, outside the U.S. at 317-572-3986, or fax 317-572-4002.

Wiley publishes in a variety of print and electronic formats and by print-on-demand. Some material included with standard print versions of this book may not be included in e-books or in print-on-demand. If this book refers to media such as a CD or DVD that is not included in the version you purchased, you may download this material at http://booksupport.wiley.com. For more information about Wiley products, visit www.wiley.com.

Library of Congress Cataloging-in-Publication Data

Names: Coggins, Celine, author.
Title: How to be heard : ten lessons teachers need to advocate for their
  students and profession / Celine Coggins.
Description: San Francisco, CA : Jossey-Bass, 2017. | Includes
  bibliographical references and index.
Identifiers: LCCN 2017026365 (print) | LCCN 2017012891 (ebook) | ISBN
  9781119374008 (pdf) | ISBN 9781119374046 (epub) | ISBN 9781119373995 (pbk.)
Subjects: LCSH: Teacher participation in administration. | Communication in
  education. | Educational leadership.
Classification: LCC LB2806.45 (print) | LCC LB2806.45 .C64 2017 (ebook) | DDC
  371.2/011—dc23
LC record available at https://lccn.loc.gov/2017026365

Cover design by Wiley

FIRST EDITION

PB Printing   10 9 8 7 6 5 4 3 2 1

For my mom and my daughters

CONTENTS

, , ,

> , , ,

ABOUT THE AUTHOR

DR. CELINE COGGINS FOUNDED TEACH PLUS IN 2007 TO EMPOWER excellent, experienced teachers to take leadership over key policy and practice issues that affect their students' success. Under Celine's leadership, Teach Plus has introduced groundbreaking programs and built a nationwide network of over twenty-six thousand teachers.

Celine started her career as a middle school teacher in Worcester, Massachusetts. She went on to become a special assistant to the Massachusetts commissioner of education, working on a set of initiatives to improve teacher quality. Celine completed her PhD at Stanford University and also holds degrees from Boston College and the College of the Holy Cross. A recognized expert on teacher leadership, Celine is a frequent invited speaker on the topic both nationally and internationally, and appears regularly in media outlets such as the *New York Times,* the *Wall Street Journal,* and the *Atlantic.* She holds an appointment as an Entrepreneur in Residence at Harvard University. She is the author of more than two dozen reports and journal articles and the editor of three prior books.

FOREWORD

FEW PROFESSIONS ARE MORE IMPORTANT TO OUR NATION'S FUTURE THAN teaching. Teachers support students' growth as they develop into well-rounded, engaged members of our society who are prepared to lead thriving lives and give back to their communities. Teachers spark students' curiosity about learning. And teachers play a vital role in ensuring that our nation lives up to its promise as a land of opportunity where, with a good education, hard work, and determination, all of our people—regardless of race, background, or circumstance—can choose their path to fulfillment and success.

Especially in recent years, a movement in education has been growing around the notion of teacher leadership. This is the simple, yet powerful idea that teachers should be valued *both* as the foremost authorities in instruction *and* as leaders who inform the development of policies that can drive improvements in the education system and student outcomes. It is also the idea that teachers should not have to leave the profession they love in order to exercise leadership in strengthening it.

For years, I have been impressed by Teach Plus, an organization that understands educators are the real experts at how policy gets translated in classrooms. Teach Plus has done incredible work to identify and develop teacher leaders who can advocate for school-level change, advance solutions to policy problems, and advise peers through professional development that they create and lead.

While I served as Secretary of Education under President Barack Obama, the Department of Education, along with ASCD, the National Board for Professional Teaching Standards (NBPTS), and other nongovernmental organizations, furthered a teacher leadership initiative called

Teach to Lead, which continues today. I am proud of the projects that thousands of educators have led individually and in cohorts as part of this work—which includes hundreds of action plans for education improvements in schools, districts, states, and across the nation.

Organized efforts such as Teach Plus and Teach to Lead are critical in continuing to build a movement of educator empowerment throughout America. Also important is that individual teachers understand how to take up the mantle of teacher leadership and how to leverage their expertise and voices in ways that can have the greatest impact.

This book is a how-to guide to do just that, but not only for teachers. It also is an invaluable resource for anyone seeking to advocate for the excellent education that all our children deserve.

As Celine Coggins points out in the following pages, all advocacy is personal. Before you can even hope to make the changes you seek, you have to understand your "why"—the thing that drives you.

For me—as a former teacher, principal, education leader at the state and national levels, and now, as an advocate with The Education Trust—the "why" always has been about ensuring that every student has access to the transformational and life-saving power of great teachers in great schools.

By the time I was 12 years old, both of my parents passed away due to illness. It was because of the support, encouragement, inspired teaching, and love of my New York City public school teachers that I made it through that difficult period and do the work I do today.

Teachers saved my life. And, every day, I know there are educators who are doing the same thing for students in classrooms all over our country. They do this even as they deliver instruction, facilitate engaging classroom lessons, master technology, analyze student work and data on student performance, and, increasingly, take on new leadership roles.

To ensure that teacher leadership is an achievable and sustainable endeavor for all teachers, it is essential that schools, districts, and states support teachers with resources and provide educators with the time and opportunities to lead. That might mean the chance to serve as peer mentors and coaches, the creation of career ladders, and the space to sit at the decision-making table.

But as you will learn in this book, if you strive to be a teacher leader, it is not enough to simply know your "why," or to create or take advantage of a leadership role. To be influential and impactful, you also need to understand the context, constraints, and opportunities of policy.

Fortunately, our nation's new education law, the Every Student Succeeds Act, includes provisions that ensure teachers can meaningfully contribute to decisions that affect the work they do with students each day.

For this reason, and because of conversations that will undoubtedly be started as a result of this book, it is an exciting time for teacher leadership in America.

As you deepen your commitment to teacher leadership or consider this work for the first time, I want to encourage you to do two things: lead on behalf of equity and lead on behalf of democracy.

The first entails focusing your efforts on closing opportunity gaps for low-income students, English learners, students of color, and students with disabilities that result in academic achievement gaps— which separate these students from their classmates and deny them the chance to achieve their dreams.

Historically underserved students have less access to quality preschool, advanced coursework, great teachers, and safe schools. They also are suspended and expelled at higher rates than their more advantaged peers. These disparities contribute to cycles of underachievement and lost potential for our children. That is why we need teachers to lead on behalf of equity. We need your leadership to right these wrongs and to address the challenges of our most vulnerable students, including homeless and foster youth and those involved in the juvenile justice system. We need your leadership to ensure that all students receive the resources and supports necessary for them to thrive.

Our nation also needs you to lead on behalf of democracy. This work entails preparing students for good citizenship so that they may become the next generation of thinkers and doers who will strengthen our communities and our country.

Leading on behalf of democracy means providing students with knowledge of civics, history, and social studies. It means nurturing students' ability to discern fact from fiction, to read and listen critically, to convey well-reasoned arguments grounded in evidence, and to understand and appreciate the perspectives and experiences of people who may be different from them. It means encouraging students to exercise their civic duties through service learning. And it means teaching them about the importance of voting and standing up for causes that matter to them.

The choices that teachers make about how to lead and lift their voices, to a large extent, determine the success of our students and our education system. As a nation, we also need to create clearer, stronger paths to capitalize on teachers' energy, expertise, and ideas—and, ultimately, elevate a profession that is central to all children achieving the American Dream.

—**John King,**
president and CEO of *The Education Trust;*
former U.S. Secretary of Education

ACKNOWLEDGMENTS

THE STORIES OF THIS BOOK ARE MOSTLY THE STORIES OF EDUCATORS I've had the pleasure of interacting with through Teach Plus. Sharing late nights with teachers studying policy, visiting their classrooms, and talking about their limitlessly unpredictable students are the highlights of my work life. Teachers like Marilyn Rhames, Abby Taylor, and Jacob Pactor have inspired me with their commitment to kids and to breaking down the barriers that stand in the way of their success. I feel privilege and responsibility in sharing their stories.

Writing this book was a team effort at Teach Plus. The entire staff was my writing accountability group. Each Friday, I committed to sending my progress in an all-staff email. Each week, I got questions, comments, and corrections back in return. The final chapters are infinitely better for this feedback. Special thanks goes to my cofounder, Monique Burns Thompson, as well as Anya Grottel-Brown, Lindsay Sobel, Paul Toner, and Will Wiggins.

I owe my ability to translate between teacher-speak and policy-speak to the best policy mentors in the country. David Driscoll, Paul Reville, Hon. George Miller, Milbrey McLaughlin, Joan Talbert, and Linda Darling-Hammond have all shaped my worldview on policy and contributed in various ways to this book.

I am grateful that many of my favorite memories of writing this book will be of working alongside my school-age daughters as they did their homework. I was never writing about something abstract. My motivation to be a good role model to them was intertwined with my motivation to contribute to improving schools while there is still time to impact their age cohort. They were my celebration committee at the conclusion of each writing stage and my all-too-opinionated focus group on cover designs. They are my purpose and my joy.

My decision to take on the risk of writing my first book was made infinitely easier knowing that my husband would support me, succeed or fail. I love you, Randy Wambold. I cannot imagine this process without you tirelessly fixing the printer, relentlessly teasing me about my love of "sets of ideas," and teaching me the meaning of words I use imprecisely. To be married to the person you admire and respect most in the world is life's greatest gift.

PREFACE

I WROTE THIS BOOK DURING A TIME OF TRANSITION IN US SOCIETY. WHEN I began, President Obama was in office, and the smart money was on Hillary Clinton becoming his successor. I finished the book in the days surrounding President Trump's inauguration. If teachers were concerned that leaders weren't listening in the previous era, that feeling has heightened with the entering administration. This is certainly a moment for teachers to learn to raise their voices.

However, this is not a book about learning to yell louder. Influencing the decisions that affect your classroom involves developing new skills, knowledge, and relationships. This is the playbook for getting started on that advocacy path. It will help you become more savvy about which issues to take on and how to best use your limited time to have an impact that will benefit your students.

We do not know what the future holds for the education agenda in America. In truth, we can never be sure in advance. Yet there are a few certainties that guide this book and make me optimistic about the role of teachers in keeping that future bright.

One of these certainties is that our students, especially our most vulnerable students, need us to act. For undocumented students, the threat of deportation now looms large. Basic agreement on the role of the federal government in supporting special needs students may now be in question. Funding cutbacks have been proposed. Teachers know best what the true costs of such changes would be in our schools, and need to be at the table to defend against them.

Another certainty is that very little education decision making happens in Washington DC. Even though the spotlight always shifts to the federal government with the arrival of a new president, most of the power to set direction in education resides at the state and local levels. The 2015 Every Student Succeeds Act pushed much more decision making away from the federal government and closer to schools. A mantra of the Trump administration is that education should be handled at the state and local levels. As states and districts work to design new, locally relevant policies, there will be opportunities for teacher participation.

A final certainty is that the voice of teachers matters. At a moment when many citizens are seeking moral authority figures around whom to mobilize, teachers have natural leadership potential. The public generally has high trust in teachers, and parents see teachers as a valuable source of information. If you take the leap to advocate for an issue you are passionate about, others will follow.

CHAPTER ONE

Storytelling

LESSON
Advocacy Starts with Your Why

I always wanted to be a teacher. I was the kid who, like so many of us, lined up my dolls and taught them math before I knew how to add. My parents were both teachers (my dad until retirement). My grandma taught kindergarten. In the lax, hippie-ish 1970s, my mom used to drop preschool-age me off for Grandma to babysit in her classroom. My grandma had a piano in her class. She'd play it, and I got to sing along with the big kids. Oh, school, you had me at that happy, off-key hello.

I never contemplated any job but teaching, and I thought my parents knew this heading into our first conversation about my college plans when I was sixteen. My dad had just taken me on my first college tour and sat me down with my mom as soon as we got home. So, they asked, what do you think you'll study in college? Wow, here was my shining moment to make them so proud! (Maybe they'd even let me borrow the car later!) "I want to study education and be a teacher," I beamed back, fully expecting them to pat me on the back and welcome me into the family business.

The gap between my expectations and reality in that conversation was a big determinant of the course of the rest of my life. My mom started to cry, and my dad started to yell. There was talk about how they must have let me down to have not exposed me to other options. They threatened that they wouldn't pay for college if I went into teaching. Didn't I want a more financially secure life? My loans would be too big to pay back on a teacher's salary. Ultimately, the message they repeated that day and for years after was, "Teaching is not for smart and ambitious people." It was the most insane, depressing, and surprising thing I'd ever heard. They were my role models, and they were teachers. They were my role models *because* they were teachers.

I didn't believe that message then, and I don't believe it now. The work of my life has been showing it to be wrong. But I've met hundreds of second- and third-generation teachers whose teacher parents gave them the same message. Every time I work with a new group of teachers, I ask if any have educator parents who discouraged them from teaching. Every group has at least one. They are not unique. In a recent study of fifty-three thousand teachers, 70 percent said they were unlikely or very unlikely to recommend teaching as a career. Only 2.7 percent said they'd encourage it.[1] The 2015 winner of a $1 million worldwide prize for teaching excellence used her platform to discourage others from entering teaching.[2]

I wrote this book because of my belief in the power of teachers and teaching. My day job, running a nonprofit focused on teacher leadership, is amazing because I get to meet hundreds of incredible teachers from all over the country every year. I am humbled by their work ethic and inspired by the stories of how they solve problems with their colleagues and for their kids. Many of those stories appear in this book. These teachers see how our schools and the teaching profession need to change to meet the challenges kids face in the twenty-first century, and they are making change happen in an outdated system that often works against them. I want to spread these stories and help other teachers become leaders in improving how schools work for students.

The core belief that drives both this book and my professional life is, *If we're going to change the teaching profession to better serve kids, especially the poor students and students of color whom our system has let down in the past, teachers need to be the leaders of that change.*

The vision that animates this work is of a true profession where teachers are the indispensible leaders of problem solving in the field, where *smart* and *ambitious* are the first words used to describe teachers. It is a vision in which great teachers stay for more than the now-typical three-year stint through a dynamic career that marries teaching with leadership. This vision has student growth *and* teacher growth at its center. This vision of our education system is achievable. Only teachers can get us there.

What Is Your *Why?*

We all have an instinct to seek our own vision of a better world—for our students, for our own children, for ourselves. Advocacy is personal. Finding your voice on any issue starts with tapping into why you care. Communicating *why* you care matters. The *why* is an expression of your values and an invitation for others to connect to them. The *why* is what motivates you to persevere through challenges.

Here's the *why* that motivated me to write the book.

Teachers across America are a diverse group, yet they are unified by a common and palpable frustration. They have lost their voice in the decisions that affect their students. This book is for every teacher who wants to reverse this damaging trend.

Evidence of this professional frustration is all around us. In a 2014 survey of twenty thousand teachers, a mere 2 percent felt that the opinions of "teachers like me" were heard and valued in national education decision making.[3] In the ten-year period from 2003 to 2012, teachers' feelings of autonomy in six key areas of decision making, such as curriculum and teaching techniques, decreased precipitously in every demographic group and every type of school.[4] Most teachers would say that nobody is listening to them. There is plenty of evidence suggesting they're right.

> Most teachers would say that nobody is listening to them. There is plenty of evidence suggesting they're right.

It does not need to be this way, and there are important exceptions to this narrative. I founded Teach Plus in 2007 and began offering a policy fellowship to excellent teachers to give them the skills and knowledge to play an influential role in education decision making. The view for teachers in our network looks different from the norm. Consider the events of just the past year or so:

- In late 2015, student testing had become a national flashpoint. President Obama was planning to speak on the issue, but first wanted to discuss it with two current teachers. I got the call to send well-informed teachers to meet with him.

- A few months later, fifty teachers gathered to celebrate their recognition as state teachers of the year for their respective home states. Two of them had been trained in our program. Every year for the past seven, at least one of our fellows has been selected for this honor.

- Only twenty-five "negotiators" in all of the United States were selected to help establish the rules for states on the new Every Student Succeeds Act to replace No Child Left Behind. Two were teachers. One was trained in our program.

In seven locations around the country, teachers whom our team has trained are taking equally important seats at decision-making tables in their states and districts. They are running for leadership roles in their unions, helping forge changes in their contracts and state laws, and launching innovative programs that improve student achievement in struggling schools. They are changing the lives of their students and, at the same time, using their daily experiences in the classroom to change the world.

Their sense of empowerment stands in stark contrast to most teachers—but so does their understanding of how the system works. I believe that if more teachers knew what these teachers knew, we could spark a revolution in teacher empowerment.

> I believe that if more teachers knew what these teachers knew, we could spark a revolution in teacher empowerment.

When education decisions are made without teachers at the table, students suffer the consequences. Since my time as a classroom teacher, I have spent the past two decades trying to figure out what teachers need to know and be able to do to influence the decisions that affect their classrooms. This book is a summary of what I have learned. It is for every teacher who wants to be a voice for students and for the teaching profession.

The Story of My Path to Teaching

So how did I get from where I was when I heard my parents' message to here? I'll use this chapter to share more of my own story as modeling for connecting a personal *why* to being a catalyst for change on a specific issue.

Instead of trying drugs or dating the wrong guys, my act of youthful rebellion was taking education courses and eventually student teaching as an undergrad. I probably got away with it only because my dad was too distracted to notice, given how dramatically all of our lives changed before the start of my sophomore year of college. My mom lost her six-year battle with cancer that summer, adding pressure to my career choice. If I went into teaching, I would be doing the one thing she had hoped I wouldn't.

Of course, I did. I became a teacher of sixth-grade earth science and eighth-grade geography. I loved the magic that surrounded us when I could close my classroom door to the rest of the world and focus on just my students. But, after a few years, I came to understand the message my parents were trying to communicate. There were few opportunities for career growth or recognition of success in teaching, few chances to connect with colleagues, and few ways to have a larger voice in addressing what my students needed.

My role today is as a teacher of policy, helping current teachers understand and influence the larger system. Although my K–12 teaching experience was a formative element of the worldview I bring to this book, I am writing as a current policy wonk and leader of a big fan club for teachers (Teach Plus). I am not a K–12 teacher today and haven't been for the better part of two decades. After leaving the classroom, I spent my first ten years in the policy world observing the gap between teachers and the people making decisions about their classrooms. I did everything I could to understand how policy worked and why teachers were so rarely at the table. Then I founded Teach Plus. For the past ten years, with a team of awesome world-changers, I've lived in that breach that separates teachers from policymakers. This book is a view from the gap between the two worlds.

The Story of My Path into Policy

August 14, 1998, was a day that changed the direction of my life. Since March of that year, I had been diligently sending applications to every middle school in the Boston Public Schools, hoping to make a move from my current position in Worcester, Massachusetts. I met David Driscoll, the commissioner of education in Massachusetts, at a low moment, and spouted off at him about my great frustration that hiring timelines were so late—it was August 14!!—and I didn't have a job yet for the fall. He invited me to come work with him on a new set of teacher quality initiatives. Once I said yes, the teaching interviews started coming in, but I had already sealed my fate.

I rationalized taking the job, thinking that I would have the chance to impact the lives of many more students by working in policy. That thought excited me. What I didn't realize was that taking on a role in influencing the lives of many would mean losing the deep relationships with individual students that were the best part of my teaching life. That trade-off is huge, and I think many teachers exiting for policy are surprised by the contrast in work environments and the depersonalized nature of policy. That's why I've made it my mission to create paths that allow teachers to stay in the classroom and also have a voice in policy. Decision makers need to hear more from actual practitioners. Teachers should not need to leave the classroom to have a larger voice.

The Lessons I Learned Transitioning from Teaching to Policy

My transition from teaching to policy was a culture shock. I learned three fundamental lessons that year that shape my work as a translator between teachers and policymakers to this day.

Lesson 1: Teachers Are Rarely Invited to the Policymaking Table

You might have suspected this, but not had any evidence. It's true.

When I was special assistant to the commissioner, my desk was very close to his office. I had the privilege of joining him in many meetings and rarely met a current, or even former, teacher in these rooms. Our relationship developed around one question that he asked me often:

"Celine, you were a teacher. What do teachers think about _____?" You could fill in that blank with any education initiative du jour, from charter schools, to the new state tests, to the changes to teacher certification and teacher leadership on which my work was focused.

If he asked what teachers thought about alternative routes to certification—the program I was working on—I'd tell him they loved it. That wasn't because I knew how they felt one way or another. It was because I wanted to keep my job. On most topics, though, I'd feel guilty about responding on behalf of actual teachers when I was sitting there in an office job. I'd put the question back on him: "Why don't you just ask teachers who are still in the classroom?"

The question made him frown a bit, evidence of a bind he had no easy way of undoing. He grumbled a bit and then explained that talking with teachers didn't help and sometimes made things worse. They had many things that they wanted from him, and most of them were impossible for him to give in light of budget and legal constraints and of rules that came from the federal government.

I believe that he wished he could answer the question differently. He came to his role via a traditional path, and his resume checked all of the boxes educators traditionally care about: longtime math teacher, followed by principal, district superintendent, then commissioner with the state Department of Education.

He was looking to make the pressing decisions that his role demanded, and teachers would inevitably come looking for something else.

Recognizing that policymakers and teachers rarely talked was one of my clearest lessons in transitioning from the classroom to policy. Part of that lesson was recognizing that policymakers actually wanted to know what teachers thought. Like my boss the commissioner, most knew that teachers' perspectives were needed to make good decisions about districts and schools. But at the same time, they saw getting those perspectives as risky and slow, and as likely to cause new problems as it was to solve the ones already on their plates.

Lesson 2: Policy Influence Doesn't Come from Telling the Story of Your Class but from Solving Other People's Problems

When I was a newbie to the policy world, one of my first assignments was to help secure funding for teacher leadership, specifically for mentoring programs that supported new teachers. My role was to meet with legislators and other stakeholders, share my experiences as a recent teacher who saw the value of this type of support, and outline the Department of Education's plan for rolling out a new statewide program. We had built a $6 million budget for recruiting, selecting, and training teacher leaders as mentors and paying them a stipend for their extra work. I needed to make the case for that line item staying in the final state budget.

I could not have been a bigger believer in the work I was doing. I had had an informal mentor in my first year in the classroom and had concrete ideas about what worked and what did not work. I saw my job as one of sharing the details of classroom life to help others understand its challenges, and the possibilities of strong induction for helping a novice teacher overcome those challenges.

I struggled mightily in meeting after meeting. Although the folks on the other side of the table were polite and nominally interested in the stories of my middle schoolers and my early struggles as a teacher, the questions they asked were at a fundamentally different level than I was prepared to address. I was operating at the school level, and they were operating at the system level. They were interested in my responses on issues like these:

- Are you proposing a tax hike to pay for this? If not, what would you cut from the current budget?

- In which locations would you start, and how would you scale the program?

- Is that really enough money to do all that you are proposing? Are program costs expected to go up or down over time?

- How will we make sure the best teachers are mentors and that new teachers are paired with experts in the same subject?

- How will we know if the program is working? What does the research from other places tell us?

I was under the mistaken impression that my job as an advocate was to help people understand my job as a teacher. In fact, the job I needed to be doing was essentially the opposite. I needed to equip legislators to do *their* job—balancing budgets, assuring constituents that tax dollars are spent wisely, ensuring that resources are distributed equitably across the system. Without my help in answering *their* questions in the context of my classroom experience, they would lack the ammunition they needed to advance the cause about which I cared so deeply. I failed to make my case on their terms, and the line item never made it into the budget.

I learned that policymakers have a limited set of tools at their disposal to help teachers. I should have had a clear understanding of what those tools were and how to leverage them. You will by the end of the book. For now, just recognize that everyone—you, other teachers, policymakers across the table—has some level of self-interest. Most often, helping others solve their problems is a big step on the path to solving your own.

Lesson 3: There Is an Invisible Policy "Playing Field" That Most Teachers Need Help Recognizing

Everything felt foreign during my first year out of the classroom. After all, I was the girl who only ever dreamed of being a teacher. What I remember most about that time was stepping into the shower each morning and having an imaginary Talking Heads soundtrack playing "How did I get here?" in my head. I missed my kids.

We talked about kids every day at the Department of Ed, but it was a global group, Kids with a capital *K*. The Kids had no actual names. The people in these conversations weren't picturing individuals—maybe the one with the first signs of a moustache, another with frizzy hair you just wanted to pull into a ponytail—when they talked about Kids. It was not at all like a faculty meeting about actual kids with names. We talked about research on Kids. We talked about stretching dollars to reach Kids.

Then, just like my former sixth graders who returned to me for eighth grade, fully assimilated into the adult bodies that were just taking form two years earlier, I became assimilated into the policy world. I didn't have real kids with real names to talk about in real time anymore. I had a deep, system-level understanding of Kids and the ways state and district decision making can help or hurt their chances of success.

Much as I hated to say it and have spent my life fighting against it, I came to understand the reasons that teachers were often excluded from the table. That they were still bothered me, yet I had become immersed in the mind-set and unspoken rules of policy. I came to see that there is an invisible playing field on which policymaking takes place, and in most cases, teachers cannot recognize it. It is the realm of the capital *K* Kids.

When you finish this book, you should have a working understanding of what policy is. Yes, much of policy will always be feeling in the dark, but you will know how to make meaning of the contours.

My description of the policy playing field will focus on the three key pressures every policymaker faces:

- **Equity.** The responsibility of the public education system is to provide *all* students an opportunity for success.

- **Resource scarcity.** Public needs will always be greater than the availability of public funds.

- **Accountability.** Given limited resources, it is important to know whether public funds are being used to yield the best possible school experience for *all* kids.

To summarize, I share this sentence that we use in our training: "Policy is the process of determining **who** gets **what** resources, **when, where,** and **how**."

As a final note about the policy playing field, I'd like to point out that I use the terms *policymakers* and *decision makers* interchangeably and as shorthand for many different people in many different roles. The terms are intended to be broad so that you can apply them to your own circumstances. They encompass district superintendents and other central office administrators; school committee members; state legislators and other state officials; and nonprofit, think tank, and philanthropic influencers. My use of the term decision maker in relation to system-level issues is in no way meant to suggest that teachers are not decision makers. Instead, it is to point out that there are government structures in place that privilege others with decision making and budgetary authority.

The Story of My Path to Supporting Teachers

I pursued my PhD in education policy to make sense of the gap between policy and practice. It was my good fortune to have Milbrey McLaughlin, Linda Darling Hammond, and Joan Talbert—the true masters—as my advisers. What I learned was that lots of people cared about teacher leadership and teacher professionalism.

In my studies, I gravitated toward a particular defining feature of what it means to be a professional. One attribute that distinguishes professions from other types of work is that *practitioners* are the ones to solve the big challenges that exist in the field. Teacher professionalism—and the improved status and influence that it entails—hinges on teachers asserting their authority as experts. We can't fix schools without teachers, true professionals, leading the way. This notion is both obvious and wildly controversial.

What I also learned in grad school was that there were very few organizations focused on expanding teacher leadership opportunities and getting teachers to the decision-making table. In launching Teach Plus, I set out to create opportunities for teachers to be leaders in solving the problems that face education at all levels of the system. Through our policy fellowship, we select, train, and activate teacher leaders to advance solutions to policy problems at the district, state, and even federal levels. We also offer a separate *instructional* leadership track for teachers who want to lead their peers through professional development and school-level change.

Over the past five years, the growth of a movement around teacher leadership has become a key positive strand of the school improvement narrative. Amid plenty of challenges, teachers have begun to lead in places and in numbers never seen in the past: districts around the nation are now negotiating teacher leadership into contracts; superintendents, state commissioners of education, and civic organizations are enlisting teachers as advisors; unions are finding new ways for teachers to own their work through teacher-led professional development; and the focus of federal education efforts has turned to teacher leadership and ensuring effective teachers for all students. I am proud of our organization's catalytic effect and grateful to the teachers who have taken up the call to lead.

During the 2015–16 school year alone, more than twelve thousand teachers participated in our teacher leadership training or one of the activities offered to our network. Although the number of participants has grown rapidly in a short time, it still represents a fraction of the teaching force. For our students' sake, the teacher leadership movement must spread.

What Should You Expect in the Pages to Come?

I hope that every teacher reads this book. I intend it as a commonsense explanation of the universe *outside* of school that affects nearly everything that happens *inside* a school. I hope this book is used to drive a fresh conversation in unions and among those taking on new teacher leadership roles—most of whom have never spent time on "the other side," the side they are seeking to influence. Too often teachers feel they need to leave the classroom to get the knowledge necessary to fight for system-level changes. That's the opposite of what should be happening. My aim is to make it more possible for current teachers—the real experts—to see the entry points for using their teacher voice to change the way education policy is made, without leaving the classroom.

My aim is to create a book that is a one-stop shop for teachers who are interested in learning about the big picture that affects their classroom, and how they can affect it right back. You might use it to figure out how to incorporate five minutes of advocacy into your life each week, or you might use it to become the next Al Shanker, transforming the role and power of teachers for generations to come.

The book is one part Policy and Advocacy 101 textbook, one part how-to guide, and one part memoir of my decade in the trenches working to get teachers a place at the table.

Policy and advocacy textbook This is the nuts-and-bolts information that is effectively the price of admission to credibly participating in policy conversations. This knowledge makes the difference between feeling around in the dark about what matters and what it is possible to change, and standing squarely on the policy playing field. It involves history, research, and description of how the policy process works.

How-to guide Beyond basic knowledge, I've added lots of concrete ideas for how to engage in decision making. They are examples from other teachers who have succeeded. To some extent, I worry that in today's polarized reform debates, many teachers might worry that doing anything other than fighting against all changes is selling out. I think that's a bad thing. Politics and policy are, by definition, an exchange of ideas, a give-and-take that involves compromise. To be sensitive to the current climate, I've highlighted a bunch of examples as "non-sellout strategies" for taking action on the policy playing field.

Memoir   I'm aware that some folks start to nod off at the mere mention of policy, so I've added lots of juicy stories that bring to life the humanness of the process and the power of regular teachers. Most of the teachers I've worked with, who have sparked real changes in their districts and states, are, like me, somewhat reluctant activists. They saw a need on behalf of their kids, then through our training saw their path to making a difference, and then they couldn't help but attempt to follow that path. That path never ends up being linear, so getting changes across the finish line sometimes feels like living in an episode of the Netflix political drama *House of Cards*.

There are many new communities of teachers emerging that seek to have a voice in education policy. They are generating much enthusiasm, especially among newer teachers, but most have not yet been able to translate that into concrete changes in districts and states. This book should offer a missing piece for aspiring teacher advocates who want to understand the audiences that their advocacy must persuade. I hope it sparks many more groups of teachers to form around the country and take action on behalf of their students.

The lessons and strategies described in the following chapters are intended to expose you to what happens on the other side of the decision-making table. If you're worried that this book isn't for you because your driving passion is social justice or personalized learning or charter schools or special education, ask yourself this question: *Is there someone or some group in charge of the rules and holding the purse strings, determining how this issue plays out in my classroom?* If your answer is yes, then you've come to the right place.

Key Takeaways

☐ Influence starts with storytelling, and storytelling starts with your *why*.

☐ Although 98 percent of teachers report that no one is listening to them, there are powerful exceptions to this rule.

☐ Teachers are rarely invited to the policymaking table.

☐ Policy influence doesn't come from telling the stories of your class, but from solving other people's problems.

☐ There is an invisible policy "playing field" that most teachers need help recognizing.

Notes

1. Tim Elmore, "Why Teachers Don't Recommend Teaching," *Growing Leaders,* February 16, 2016, http://growingleaders.com/blog/teachers-dont-recommend-teaching/?utm_content=&utm_medium=email&utm_name=&utm_source=govdelivery&utm_term=.
2. Randi Weingarten, "How the Teacher Shortage Could Turn into a Crisis," *Huffington Post,* April 16, 2016, http://www.huffingtonpost.com/randi-weingarten/how-the-teacher-shortage_b_9712286.html.
3. Margery Mayer and Vicki Phillips, *Primary Sources: America's Teachers on Teaching in an Era of Change* (New York: Scholastic Education 2014), http://www.scholastic.com/primarysources/teachers-on-teaching.htm.
4. Dinah Sparks, John Ralph, and Nat Malkus, *Public School Autonomy in the Classroom* (Washington, DC: National Center for Education Statistics, 2015), http://nces.ed.gov/pubs2015/2015089.pdf.

CHAPTER · TWO
Expertise

LESSON
There Are No Experts

I magine a fancy room at a Washington, DC think tank. White tablecloths cover a group of eight-person round tables, there's a swanky breakfast spread on a buffet off to the side, and the topic for the day's meeting—The Challenge of Modernizing Teaching—is projected on multiple screens with a high-end tech setup.

One of my favorite things to do in my job is bring classroom teachers from cities around the country to attend meetings like this on the subject of their profession. It is an exercise in perspective for all involved. These meetings take place fairly often at organizations that focus on education policy. Perhaps not surprisingly, current practicing teachers, historically speaking, have rarely been in attendance at these meetings. Most often, for legitimate and practical reasons—the meetings are held during the school day and an airplane ride away from most US schools—teachers had been represented by union staff members.

I had attended these types of meetings wearing my policy hat for years, and when things got boring, as they inevitably did, I would pass the time amusing myself by imagining what actual teachers would think if they were in the room listening to people talk about their profession. Eventually, I decided to figure out how to make that happen.

So now there's an alternate universe where great teachers are holding their own at these tables. We've helped teachers push in through Teach Plus. The differences are substantive (teachers bring different ideas and challenges to the conversation) and subtle. (It is a positive indicator of the stature of a profession when expert practitioners are flown to Washington to consult with government leaders.) I'll never forget chatting with Shelli Shaddy, a Chicago teacher, between her early morning flight and the start of one such session. She described how her seatmate on the plane asked her whether she was flying for business or pleasure. When she replied business, he asked her line of work. Telling me her reply, she had a look of unequivocal joy and pride: "I'm a teacher." Yes! This! This needs to become the norm.

At this point, I've brought dozens of teachers from all over the country to these types of meetings, but having teachers in attendance is still the exception and not the rule. Upon entering the room, these teachers always react the same way. First, they politely ask how many of the participants are current teachers, and I reply none. Then they ask, *Who are these people, and what do they do all day?!*

Great question. To get to the answer, I first want to zoom out and take the widest possible look at our education system.

The Blind Men and the Elephant

On my first day of grad school, one of my favorite professors, Larry Cuban, introduced the study of education policy using the ancient story of the blind men and the elephant. As the story goes, a group of blind men seek to learn about an elephant, but each one touches a different part. One feels the smooth, hard ivory of the tusk; another a pliable, wrinkly knee; a third man feels the heat and moisture at the end of the trunk; and yet another feels the big wall of the belly. When they describe what they feel, it is clear that they are having completely different experiences. There is no question that each of them is feeling what a real elephant feels like, but their own realities make it hard for them to understand the others' experience of the same elephant.

I've never found a better analogy to explain education policy and the complexity of getting the different parts of the system to speak to one another. Even when the varied actors are open to collaboration, they are all bringing their own perspective, their own reality. When it comes to our complex education system, the real, lived experiences of some individuals will always be at odds with those of others. Take the classic debate over charter and district schools. If your only teaching experience has been in a regular district school and it has been a positive experience, of course you would be likely to believe that investing in the traditional system is best for students. If your best friend has only taught in a charter school and loved her experience equally, she is likely to be more open to charter expansion and alternative school models. Each of you has expertise. Each of you has developed an opinion based on experience and knowledge of how a part of "the system" works. But each of you is also feeling just one part of the elephant.

Because policy is about decisions that are made at the system level—by definition affecting thousands, even millions of individuals at a time—reconciling these conflicting perspectives into a coherent set of rules for how the system should unify expectations across those individuals is about as easy as getting the blind men to agree on their description of the elephant.

The Good News for Teachers in the Blind Men Story

If education policy is the elephant and all of us working to improve it are the blind men, what does that mean for teachers, specifically?

After nearly twenty years of working in education policy, I have come to believe that there is no such thing as an Education Policy Expert. I have been called this more times than I can count, and I have a doctorate in education policy, but there are oceans of things that I do not know about education. Most often, when I meet teachers, they are somewhat intimidated to participate in policy conversations because they believe they lack expertise. What they don't know—and need to know—is that *everyone* in the conversation lacks expertise.

There are people working in government offices who are expert in understanding the interplay of education laws at the local, state, and federal levels. There are people working alongside them who are expert in budgeting to ensure an equitable distribution of limited education dollars. There are people from the nonprofit sector who are expert in navigating effective partnerships between outside partners and school districts. There are experts in community organizing who help disadvantaged students and their families fight for better schools. There are experts in charter schools; there are academics, and there are experts in building effective philanthropic partnerships with schools. There are experts in administration occupying roles in districts and state departments of education. Varied constellations of these "policy people" are the ones in the room for the meeting I described at the start of the chapter.

And there are experts on how policy gets translated into classrooms across America. These people are teachers. Their perspective is important in policymaking. Teachers, as policy researchers Weatherley and Lipsky famously pointed out, have a unique power in policy.[1] The term they coined was *street-level bureaucrats,* linking teachers directly into the long chain of government officials associated with any policy. Because all new policies include some areas that lack specificity, "street-level bureaucrats are the policymakers." At the street level, they develop coping mechanisms and modifications that cause policy implementation to take on a distinct-looking life of its own, separate from what is written in the original law.

Teachers are the ones who control how any given policy gets implemented in the classroom, and thus they own a large part of whether it succeeds or fails. Without real teachers at the table from the outset of the policy development process, offering real-world feedback on how a theoretical idea will play out among actual children, we increase the likelihood of problems and unintended consequences, and we decrease the odds of actually improving schools. The cringe-worthy example of the last decade that I return to many times in this book is the mandate for annual student testing. It is a story of good intentions, minimal teacher participation in the early days, and, eventually, a street-level showdown called the opt-out movement.

Policy expertise is the big umbrella encompassing many domains. And teaching expertise—street-level policy implementation expertise—is one of those domains. But as any teacher knows, even teaching expertise is far from monolithic. Some teachers are deeply familiar with how special education laws affect students. Some are expert in how large-scale standards efforts like the Common Core State Standards get translated to their school context. Still others have become expert in the changing rules for schools deemed to be in "turnaround" status. Depending on whether you teach in an urban, suburban, or rural context, your understanding of how education spending affects students will be different.

So there are no real experts, and teachers have one critical form of expertise that matters in the policy discourse. Those are two important pieces of information for any teacher who picks up this book hoping to have a say in the policies that affect his or her classroom. I've got another as well: policymakers often want to hear from teachers.

Although teachers are too infrequently in the rooms where education decisions are made, many, many policymakers—from superintendents to school board members to members of the US Congress—are very interested in hearing directly from teachers. In fact, the ease I had in getting teachers on policymakers' calendars was one of my biggest positive surprises when starting Teach Plus. Before I tried, I had wondered, as many teachers do, whether the reason that teachers were so often *not* involved in policy was that important officials had built impenetrable fences around themselves. Would they not return calls and emails from actual teachers? Would they refuse meetings? Would they never consider a trip into a live classroom? When I reached out, I could not have found these assumptions to be further from the truth.

Former congressman George Miller (D-CA) served in the US House of Representatives for forty years and chaired the Education, Labor and Pensions Committee for much of that time before retiring in 2014. He now serves on the Teach Plus board of directors. He believes very deeply in teachers having a voice in policy, and he had had a longtime front-row seat to the challenge of connecting actors across levels of the system. As he tells it, "We wanted to talk to teachers, but there was no easy way to have access to the ones who were currently in the classroom. And, for them to meaningfully help us, they needed more information on the policymaking process and what was and was not possible."

The Challenging News for Teachers in the Blind Men Story

The point that George Miller makes is a significant one: although he clearly supports and encourages teacher involvement in policy, he also puts an important condition on such involvement. Congressman Miller makes clear that not every teacher was equally equipped to help him make good policy. Teachers need to know something about the policy context, the constraints under which education decisions are made, and the resources available and what various ideas cost. Without that knowledge, they are essentially planting a seed in a pile of snow. There is simply no entry point for classroom anecdotes to take root and thrive as policy.

Although the good news is that most people in the policy world want teachers at the table, I've met plenty who are quite clear about why teachers are often excluded. There is a decent-size minority in the policy community who do not think teachers *should* be at the table. Plenty of people have told me that the very idea of Teach Plus as a bridge builder between policy-makers and practitioners is Pollyannaish. Some of these people have sharp elbows. Their reasoning, in short, is that the language of policy is different than the language of practice.

To them, people who operate at the system level in their daily lives are all feeling different parts of the skin of the elephant. Teachers, in contrast, are inside, feeling the belly of the beast, and those worlds are too different for the inhabitants to talk meaningfully. This book is intended to make teachers bilingual, adding the language of policy to deep expertise in the language of practice.

To find entry points in policy, teachers must be practical. Just as you take seriously the importance of decisions you make as a teacher in the lives of your students, policymakers experience the decisions they must make as equally high pressure. The choices they make about budget and regulations affect thousands, if not millions, of children's lives. They don't have all the information they need, and you hold important pieces of the puzzle. Most of the time, though, you'll be most influential if you view your role as helping them solve *their* problems, en route to solving yours. To paraphrase the famous words of John F. Kennedy, ask not what your policymaker can do for you, but what you can do for your policymaker. That's the shortest path to the changes you want in your classroom.

Many policymakers want to hear from teachers—*if* teachers can offer viable strategies to solve real-time policy problems.

From the perspective of policy leaders, teachers who approach them simply describing what is happening in their classrooms sound like the adults in a Charlie Brown cartoon—like speakers of an unrecognizable language. Many policymakers want to hear from teachers—*if* teachers can offer viable strategies to solve real-time policy problems.

Advocacy Is Not for the Faint of Heart

Politics are a part of making policy. It can be a rough-and-tumble world of ideas. Policy is always made with imperfect information based on theories about the future or about how an idea that works in one context might translate to another. The truth is that no one knows how a specific new policy will play out in a specific context where it has never been tried. There are always an infinite number of variables that enter the equation. At the same time, there are some things that our field *does* know about how to best serve kids, and there are lessons about what works that can be gleaned from large data sets. Parsing fact from opinion at the policy table is legitimately hard and not for the faint of heart.

With the rise of social media and the blogosphere, venting about conspiracy theories and the malicious intent of "the other side" is worse than it ever was. I know this makes using one's "teacher voice" intimidating. The prospect intimidated me for a very long time because I hadn't learned the first lesson of this book: that there are no experts. I thought that someday I might speak up, but that I should wait until I had all the information. When I was experienced enough in the policy world to trust that I had information to share, I was intimidated to write a book like this about teacher voice because I was so long out of the classroom myself.

There are lots of people who hope that educators with fresh perspectives will wait and will feel either subtly or directly intimidated. But there are lots of kids who need you *not* to wait. I've lived with many teachers through their first experience of getting political pushback. It is often hard for them, and I take very seriously the responsibility of supporting teachers in these times. Most conclude pretty quickly that it is better to spark dialogue with an honest comment about their beliefs than to say something so mild that it doesn't matter.

My first piece of advice is this: pick your battles. My second is: when you do choose to fight for something controversial, recognize that if you are speaking on behalf of your real students from your real classroom experience, you have a moral authority that is unrivaled in the policy world.

> **If you are speaking on behalf of your real students from your real classroom experience, you have a moral authority that is unrivaled in the policy world.**

Over time, I've developed a super-nerdy hobby to remind myself that no matter what the policy issue, people are going to feel different sides of the elephant. After my own kids are in bed, at the top of any hour, I flip between CNN, FOX News, and MSNBC to see what they decide to run as the lead story each night and how they cover it. Spoiler alert: they never have the same take on the top story and rarely even agree on what the top story is. I'm often left wanting to throw my phone through the TV (at one station more than the others), but it's clear that the commentators are not espousing ideas I disagree with because they are evil. Understanding the motivations of different actors helps me get clear on how I might approach them, persuade them, or undermine their point of view in future conversations. Understanding the psychology and logic of "the other side" helps make it less threatening to me.

Because there are so many different domains of expertise and levels of the system, education reformers tend to break into factions that don't look or sound very different from the factions you see within a school faculty. These are echo chambers filled with people who talk frequently to like-minded people and, unsurprisingly, get reinforcement for the ideas they were already holding when they entered the conversation. Facebook and Twitter have their own "faculty rooms." We all know them. They are the groups of five friends connected in an uninterrupted loop of sharing or "favoriting" the same link. This becomes problematic because we become more deeply entrenched in the perspectives we already hold and less open to the ideas outside our echo chamber. Further, in the anonymous online world, it's easy to ascribe malicious intent to someone you will never see.

Still, I believe that there is no bad intent 99 times out of 100. (Yes, I recognize that 1 percent of people may be bad actors.) Even if you're trying to deal with that unfortunate 1 percent, you're not going to get something to change for your students if your approach begins with mistrust and pessimism.

I confess to taking the names of certain educational and political leaders in vain over the years because of my frustration with their stance, but I can honestly say something that many folks in education policy cannot: I actually reach out and try to have conversations with people I don't see eye-to-eye with, rather than assuming that they are acting intentionally against the interest of kids. You will be amazed at how far that simple step can get you.

Non-Sellout Strategy for Asserting Your POV

One of my personal heroes and writing role models is educator and blogger Marilyn Rhames, whom I had the honor of getting to know when she was a policy fellow in Chicago. She has been criticized for working in a charter school and for working with Teach Plus on controversial issues like

teacher evaluation. Her writing exemplifies the grace and wisdom of someone who decided to get involved with advocacy for the right reasons. Here is
an excerpt of her response the first time she was attacked online.

> I am relatively new to the world of education policy. I entered the
> arena two years ago through Teach Plus, a non-profit organization
> that aims to offer leadership opportunities to high quality teachers
> with at least three years urban teaching experience. Through Teach
> Plus, I have collaborated with a wide array of teachers with different
> experiences and perspectives on key issues. . . . What I didn't know
> was that I was actually entering into a boxing ring, a place where
> educated people who say they love children often beat each other up
> with words and accusations. I spend the day telling students to do the
> exact opposite, so the initial right hook from a fellow educator caught
> me totally off guard.
>
>   Normally, this wouldn't faze me, but one of my students is dead.
> He was killed early on Christmas morn because someone decided
> to drink and drive. In my grief over break, I made the mistake of
> reading education blogs and realized that anything you say can and
> most certainly WILL be used against you in the court of the educa-
> tion blogosphere. Don't get me wrong—I have very thick skin. You
> don't grow up on the South Side of Chicago, among the youngest in
> a family of ten, and then set off to pursue journalism in New York
> City without it. But I found myself at a vulnerable point when my
> precious student died. I read several rational education blog posts,
> then read pages and pages of negative comments. Then I read accu-
> satory, bitterly biting education blog posts that were followed by
> congratulatory comments. *What the hell is going on?* I asked myself,
> and I'm not the swearing kind.
>
>   I understand that lots of people have legitimate reasons to dis-
> agree with my philosophy of education. I know that neither I, nor
> Teach Plus, nor any earthly organization has all the answers about
> how to fix the terrible mess American education finds herself in. But
> I do believe that if we could somehow start listening to each other; if
> we could agree to validate good ideas, even if they are coming from
> someone we generally disagree with; if we could commit ourselves
> to a civil discourse and resist the temptation to distract from the
> important conversations through our sensational displays of resent-
> ment, then and only then would we be able to make effective, lasting
> change for our failing students.[2]

(continued)

Marilyn's writing is a textbook example of responding to criticism with professionalism and authenticity—and without backing down from her affiliations or beliefs. In her case, the pushback happened online, but you can also expect a leader with a different point of view to push back in a private meeting. Marilyn sets a model that others can follow in any clash of ideas:

1. **Take the high road.** Marilyn refrains from calling out the individuals who hurt her and offers ideas to forge better discourse.

2. **Focus on what you know—your own experience and that of your students.** That is your area of expertise, and that is what matters most.

3. **Know when to say when.** The trolls are out there and willing to engage in an unproductive back-and-forth ad infinitum if you let them. Resist!

Becoming a Better Learner, Rather Than an Expert

Never mistake the message that there are no experts as a suggestion that you have enough knowledge to be an effective policy influencer. Anyone who hopes to be an influencer must be a learner first and always. The people I admire most who get the most done in our field are those who have attempted to touch many sides of the elephant.

> Anyone who hopes to be an influencer must be a learner first and always.

Harvard professor Richard Elmore published a book comprising interviews with education leaders who have persisted over the decades, called *I Used to Think . . . And Now I Think*. Our field operates better, and our work on behalf of students is better, when we take the approach of a learner. In the best case, a person's stance evolves with new experiences. If you hope to find that type of open-mindedness in a policymaker, then you should expect the same of yourself.

There are many, many excellent, knowledgeable teachers who need opportunities to develop new skills and share from their domain of expertise. Think of the crowded and ever-growing field of celebrity chefs. At this point, every city seems to have a dozen. What they have in common is excellence in one thing (cooking) that stretched them to grow proficiency in another skill (business) in order to expand their influence and have a greater impact.

To extend the analogy, we need celebrity teachers, who never stray from the particular genius they have—teaching kids—but extend that genius into policy to drive larger changes. I have met thousands of teachers over the past decade who have a similar drive to keep honing their true calling in teaching, while also building new skills in policy to accelerate them on their path to changing the world. They have what it takes to gain influence because they are fundamentally learners. They continue to go deeper in becoming better at serving kids while also learning how to influence the larger system in which their classroom lives.

"The Party of No" versus "the Third Way"

The culture at Teach Plus among both our teachers and staff can be summed up in one phrase: solution oriented. This is a mind-set that is essential for thriving in the opaque policy world. The working definition we use for *solution oriented* is this: Transformational change is possible when we take action in the following way: (1) rigorously assess need, (2) boldly define opportunity, and (3) apply creativity, tenacity, and resourcefulness.

Too often, teachers are characterized as "the party of no" when it comes to changes in education. Sometimes that's a fair characterization; sometimes it isn't.

Sometimes opposition to change has a good reason behind it. (Street-level bureaucrats are best positioned to see how system-level ideas can play out as school-level problems.) Sometimes the logic behind resistance is less clear.

Sometimes this "party of no" moniker is associated with unions. The view I'll take here and throughout the book is this: unions play an important role in ensuring a thriving teaching force and middle class, yet they need to evolve with the times. There are incredible, solution-oriented state and local union leaders leading the way on this (a tip of the hat to, for example, Carrie Dallman in Colorado; David Lowe in New Haven,

Connecticut; and Maddie Fennell in Omaha, Nebraska), and there are others who are struggling to move into the twenty-first century. My role as an outsider is to encourage teachers who have learned how policy works to step up and be change agents within their unions. The many who have done so have been excited by the generally positive reception of their ideas. I describe many examples of this in the pages to come.

Think briefly about a student with whom you've had problems. You're not sure which battles to fight with him until you understand the root causes of his behavior. Likewise, in figuring out which policy battles to fight, you might feel blind to the larger context. By the end of the book, you will have a framework for making better-informed decisions about where to resist and where and how to be a solution-oriented participant in the process of creating good policies that serve your students.

An important part of this learning is looking for a third way. Oftentimes, positions on an issue get calcified into the "pro" camp and the "anti" camp. The most valuable people in those kinds of stalemates are the ones who can find a different angle or question that allows the problem to be redefined and new possibilities to emerge. As David Brooks puts it, "[People have] a natural tendency to narrow-frame, to see every decision as a binary 'whether or not' alternative. Whenever you find yourself asking 'whether or not,' it's best to step back and ask, 'How can I widen my options?'"[3]

The third way is the path forward that cuts through the polarization that had previously divided two sides on the issue.

Non-Sellout Strategy for Finding a Third Way

Testing: Are you for it or against it? That question has been on a lot of people's minds over the past few years. Yet a group of our Indianapolis policy fellows decided that the public discourse was focused on the wrong question.

In May 2012, third-grade teacher Laura Yates entered the session raving about how excited her students were to get back scores on their third round of computer-adaptive assessments, which showed their growth over the course of the year. One thing she said still stands out in my mind for its rarity: "When their scores came up, they were all crying; I was crying." She meant tears of joy. Seriously.

Most of the other teachers in the group couldn't relate to her excitement. They may have experienced tears—but they certainly weren't of the joyful variety. The majority of them gave just the state test, once a year, on paper. Their kids didn't know how they did until long after they'd entered the next grade. As a group of teachers with different experiences on the same topic, they recognized something missing from the testing debate: all tests aren't created equal.

They plotted a strategy for teachers to be able to have a voice in rating the assessments they gave. In doing so, they found a third way through the testing debates. They changed the question from a nonstarter in policy—Should we keep or end testing?—to one that policymakers could act on: Which tests are worth keeping, and which ones should states and districts discard?

We worked with the teachers to develop an online platform called Assessment Advisor. It worked like Trip Advisor or Yelp!, allowing teachers to rate the assessments they gave to their students. Several hundred different state and off-the-shelf assessments were available to be rated. The NEA sent news of the tool out to all of its members, and several thousand teachers gave ratings.

Ultimately, data from Assessment Advisor launched a new kind of conversation about how to improve tests. It showed, as nothing had before, how much variation teachers experienced in test quality. When hundreds of teachers rated the assessments they had given, some assessments got nearly 5 of 5 stars and others got 1 of 5 stars. On the site, teachers were also able to select reasons for their rating.

The teachers brought their findings to state leaders and even earned a meeting with the then secretary of education Arne Duncan on the topic. There is language in the new Every Student Succeeds Act encouraging states and districts to audit the tests they give and include teacher voice in the process, which mirrors the teachers' recommendations exactly. This is the power teachers have when they can offer third-way solutions to real policy problems.

Key Takeaways

☐ Every person at the education decision-making table is limited in his or her expertise and has incomplete information.

☐ Teachers have a domain of expertise that should be present at the table.

☐ Teachers have power in policy because as "street-level bureaucrats," they control policy implementation.

☐ Many policymakers want to hear from teachers—*if* teachers can offer viable strategies to solve real-time policy problems.

☐ The politics of education decision making are contentious, but that should not be a reason for teachers to be intimidated into not having a voice.

☐ Social media can be a place to link up with like-minded colleagues, but it can also magnify ideological divides.

☐ Teachers need to come to the table with solutions, not just opposition, if they want to be asked back.

Notes

1. Richard Weatherley and Michael Lipsky, "Street-Level Bureaucrats and Institutional Innovation: Implementing Special Education Reform," *Harvard Educational Review 47*, no. 2 (July 1977): 171–197.
2. Marilyn Rhames, "Our Children Are But Grass, So Let's Stop Fighting!" *Education Week Teacher* (blog), January 11, 2012, http://blogs.edweek.org/teachers/charting_my_own_course/2012/01/our_children_are_but_grass_so_lets_stop_fighting.html.
3. David Brooks, "The Choice Explosion," *New York Times,* May 3, 2016, https://www.nytimes.com/2016/05/03/opinion/the-choice-explosion.html.

CHAPTER THREE

History

LESSON
The Policies That Impact Your Classroom Are Not Random

R aise your hand if you've ever gotten word from on high about a new rule or mandate to enact in your classroom and your reaction was *What were they thinking?!* Followed closely by *Are they crazy? Have they ever been in a classroom?*

If Pinterest can count as evidence, this experience is as common as kindergarteners forgetting to wash their hands in the bathroom. Internet memes making fun of the disconnect between teachers and policymakers abound. We all love them, and (because this chapter is about to get very dry very fast) I'll include a few for illustration here. Can you relate to any of these?

- I wish a politician with no teaching experience would just come in and tell me how to teach . . . said no teacher ever.
- Paperwork is such a great use of my planning time . . . said no teacher ever.
- We don't have enough assessments. Let's create more . . . said no teacher ever.

These capture the zeitgeist among teachers. Most often, policy mandates don't make sense in the context of the classroom. They seem random or unnecessary or, in plenty of cases, misguided. It's true: sometimes they *are* unnecessary, and sometimes they *are* misguided. This chapter is not a defense of policymakers or policy ideas. However, policies do come from somewhere. They are not random.

This chapter is designed to help you understand how history, the basic characteristics of our education system, and the current political context all mix together to create a breeding ground where some ideas thrive and others wither.

From the classroom, it's easy to see the information about education that policymakers are missing. But what about putting the shoe on the other foot? What are the fundamentals of policymaking that you may not understand?

A former colleague of mine, the inimitable Casey Patterson from Indianapolis, would launch her policy fellows training for teachers with the following deceptively simple-sounding exercise: "Welcome, teachers! Turn to your table mate and name one of the state legislators who represents you." The class we were leading, of course, was made up of teachers who had applied to our program because they were interested in policy. They had been selected because they were the best in a large pool of applicants, yet almost none of them could answer the question. Could you?

Admit it. There is a lot you don't know about where (and who) decisions come from.

It is important to recognize that education policy is not the sum total of all that is happening across many schools. It is not an extension of what happens in classrooms. Education policy is a separate discipline, informed by what happens in classrooms, but only in part. It is where K–12 schools intersect with the broader political and economic context.

Start with the Same Psychology Test You Apply to Students

When it comes to students, teachers intuitively understand that the behaviors that appear in the classroom, however misguided they seem, aren't random. They are most often responses to challenges that are occurring in the students' larger world. Understanding that larger world becomes essential to helping students succeed.

It is the same with education policy. When it arrives in your classroom, it may not make much sense. As I've already noted, however, the policy is not random. (And it is typically not created—as some cynics suggest—because bad or ill-intentioned people are making the decisions.) It comes from somewhere. There is a logic to how policy is made. And just as you would do with a struggling student, understanding the bigger picture is the best way to begin to change its course.

Knowing the Fundamentals Is the Price of Admission to the Policy Table

Although no one is an expert in all aspects of policy, there is a common body of knowledge that people who work in policy tend to share. So what do the policy people know that you might not? Consider this chapter the Cliff's Notes version of a comprehensive Policy 101 textbook.

In organizing the chapter, I boiled all of the topics that I wanted to cover down to two very lengthy sentences, which I've separated into the bulleted points here:

- Schools are trying to serve a large group of students whose demographic profile is changing rapidly,
- With a teaching force whose demographic profile is changing rapidly,
- In a system that was built on tensions between local control and federal support,
- Where each level of the system plays a different role in establishing expectations and providing funding.

, , ,

- The modern era of education reform began with *A Nation at Risk* sounding an alarm in 1982,
- And our attention to standards and accountability has grown in the twenty-first century, though
- The data paint a mixed picture of progress in US schools over the past generation.

Each of these points will get its own section with further detail in this chapter. In the different sections of the narrative on US education, I've added the questions that get raised at the policy level. Be looking for the *WWPT* (What would a policymaker think?) label. You can view this chapter as Think Like a Policymaker boot camp. Before we start, I want to acknowledge that whole books have been written on each of the paragraphs in this chapter.

The Data on Students and Schools

The US education system is vast and diverse. Trying to understand it through just the half-dozen or fewer schools you have experienced will certainly result in blind spots.

Majority minority Today in the United States, there are approximately 50.1 million students in grades K–12. As of 2014, students of color became the majority in US classrooms, a trend that is expected to continue. According to current reporting categories, there are 24.7 White students and 25.4 million students of other races, including 7.7 million Black students, 13.1 million Hispanic students, 2.6 million Asian/Pacific Islander students, and 500,000 Native American students.[1]

WWPT? How should we reallocate resources to respond to the growth of the population that US schools have served least well?

No standard district or school size   There are just under 100,000 schools in the United States. Most are affiliated with one of the nation's 13,500 school districts. School districts vary widely in size: hundreds of them each serve just one school, and many of them serve hundreds of schools under one umbrella. New York City is the largest district, with seventeen hundred schools serving 1.1 million students; Los Angeles and Chicago are not far behind.[2]

WWPT? In such a diverse system, what topics should be codified in policy, and which should be left to local discretion?

The role of charters   Charter schools are a fast-growing alternative to traditional district schools. Like district schools, charter schools are public schools that receive public taxpayer dollars on a per-pupil basis. However, they have more autonomy than district-run schools, with choices around budgeting, curriculum, programs, and whether to affiliate with a union. There are sixty-one hundred charter schools in the United States, serving roughly 6 percent of all students. Despite their relatively small imprint, charter schools play an outsize role in education reform debates because the sector is growing quickly, because these schools are intended to promote innovation, and because some networks of charter schools serving high-need students are consistently outperforming their surrounding district.[3]

WWPT? How can we scale charter innovations that work?

Data and Trends in Staffing

The K–12 system employs approximately 3.1 million teachers (in Full-Time Equivalent, FTE). That averages out to a 16:1 student-teacher ratio across all schools.[4] I'm guessing that for many teachers, that ratio seems like a fantasy. I've visited plenty of teachers' classrooms over the past few years with ratios as high as 50:1, with two different math courses being taught at the same time. I note the average because it is a good example of how US education is defined by variation. There are lots of extremes hidden in that mean.

The Hidden Half

Teachers constitute only about half of the staff employed by school districts. In 2014, the Fordham Institute released a report called *The Hidden Half*, detailing how principals, district administrators, operations and tech support staff, and ever-growing numbers of coaches and instructional leaders now make up more than 50 percent of district payrolls. So as one answer to the question, "Who are all those nonteachers whose decisions affect my classroom?" more of those people than you probably realized are right there in your district or charter management organization.

> WWPT? Is the proliferation of nonteacher roles resulting in improved student outcomes?

A Historic Demographic Shift

For more than four decades—from the late 1960s until a few years ago— Baby Boomers made up the majority demographic in the teaching force. Many served full careers in the classroom, marching through together as a bloc of recent college grads in the 1960s and 1970s, then as moms and dads in the 1980s and 1990s, finally nearing retirement in the early years of this century.

A few years ago, we reached a demographic tipping point. Research I conducted with my colleague Heather Peske showed that, as of about 2008, those with ten or fewer years experience had become the majority in the teaching force. As of 2008, 51 percent of teachers had between one and ten years of experience. The emergence of this new majority is of interest to those making system-level decisions. These teachers have the potential to shape how we educate children for the next several decades. They raise questions about whether aspects of the system that relate to teachers need to change to reflect the interests of a new demographic group. Policymakers would ask questions like these:

WWPT? What incentives motivate this new majority? How are they different from and similar to their predecessors?

In a strictly democratic sense, as a group ascends into the majority, it would be expected to have greater influence. Yet there are structural reasons why it is hard for this to happen in teaching. Schools have historically operated as seniority-driven cultures. The rules (for example, for who is dismissed first in a layoff process, who is first in line for certain leadership opportunities, who gets to teach classes deemed most desirable) are set up to most benefit those with the greatest longevity. The message to young teachers is often: *Wait your turn. Accept the system as it is, and it will work for you in time.*

Shifts in Career Longevity and Expectations

Whether it is because they don't want to wait their turn to be rewarded for strong performance, or for other reasons, the incoming generation of teachers is generally not signing up for an entire career in the classroom. Like Millennials in other fields, today's teachers expect to switch jobs frequently over the course of a career, and they want to be recognized for their accomplishments with increasing levels of leadership and authority. Programs like Teach for America have also reinforced a reset on the notion of a lifelong career in the classroom—for both the public and practitioners. Whether this is a good or a bad thing for kids can be debated, but in policy terms, shorter teaching careers are a reality that must be considered.

WWPT? If teachers are not staying in the classroom for multiple decades, what recruitment and retention incentives can ensure a strong teaching force?

Federal Power and States' Rights, or Why the United States Has as Many Policy Wonks as Teachers

You may have taken a History of American Education course in your preparation program and zoned out knowing that it wouldn't really affect how you taught students. It matters now.

Local Control as the Starting Point

The US system of education is decentralized. That is, the federal government has historically had a limited role, and states and localities have been free to make most of their own rules. Schools began as local enterprises with local decision making over what would be taught, when, and how. This tradition and history of local control is alive and well in spirit in communities across the country that celebrate what is unique about their schools.

For anyone who thinks that standardization has scrubbed our desire for uniqueness out of schools, I'd offer my own example. In my kids' school each year, a mother duck nests in the school's inner outdoor courtyard. When her ducklings begin to hatch, every student in the school is dismissed from class (no matter what they are doing) to line a path for the ducks from the courtyard to a nearby pond. This past year, the duck story was covered by CNN and has had over three million views on YouTube.

The American ethos of freedom and independence was baked into formal schooling as it developed in this country. We all have a soft spot for it to this day.

WWPT? On which issues should we standardize practice, and on which should local control reign?

Inequity of Opportunity as a Constant

Inequity of opportunity is just as deeply baked into formal schooling in the United States as local control. Public schooling, and eventually compulsory school, emerged in the nineteenth century in America. But by the end of that century, in 1896, the Supreme Court ruled in *Plessy v. Ferguson* that public institutions could be "separate but equal," leading many states to pass laws segregating schools. That ruling was overturned in 1954 with *Brown v. Board of Education of Topeka,* which ruled that segregated schools were "inherently unequal." However, evidence of the legacy of institutional racism and continued inequity of opportunity is clear in enduring achievement gaps between poor students and their affluent peers and between Black and Hispanic students and their White and Asian peers. Today, schools are more segregated by race and class than they were forty years ago.[5]

The challenge of addressing equity will be taken up in more detail in chapter 5.

The Federal Role as Means of Addressing Inequity

The federal role in education is a new phenomenon, historically speaking. It was only under Lyndon Johnson in 1965 that the feds took a major, active role in funding and setting expectations for education. That was the year that the Elementary and Secondary Education Act (ESEA, later reauthorized as No Child Left Behind and later as the Every Student Succeeds Act) was first enacted into law. The US Department of Education only began operating in 1980. Federal intervention in schools began as part of the War on Poverty. Federal involvement was for a single purpose: to address the vast inequity of opportunity that students around the country were experiencing in different educational settings. The origin—and still the primary purpose—of the federal role in education is grounded in civil rights.

Figure 3.1 Conflicting Priorities at Different Levels of Education Policymaking

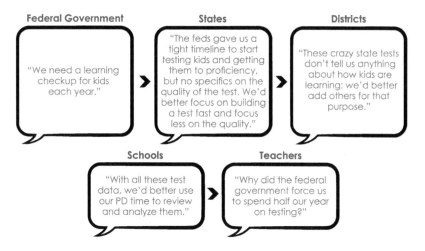

This is *very* different from most other countries. In most countries, standards and expectations are set nationally; national curriculum and national tests are taken for granted. In the United States, fifty states and 13,500 districts are figuring out where they can craft their own rules and where they must follow direction from above. Enter the administrators and policy types, the humans operating at a minimum of four different distinct levels of the system—schools, districts, states, and the federal government—navigating an interconnected (and sometimes conflicting) web of rules, budgetary requirements, and personal power struggles. It is a big, complex system in which a teacher's natural interest in treating students as individuals and adapting to meet local needs collides with a policymaker's interest in reining in what appears to be chaos (Figure 3.1).

The Levels of the System and How Money Moves through It

Funding for public schools comes from local, state, and federal taxes. The federal government is responsible for the smallest piece of the funding pie by far. For the past three decades or so, the federal contribution hovered just under 10 percent of the total education budget. The federal role grew, and the contribution has risen to 12 percent in the past few years. The remaining 90-ish percent is split evenly between the state contribution and the local contribution. However, towns that are more affluent (with greater property tax revenues) tend to pick up a larger percentage of the total education bill than the state. In lower-income areas, the local contribution tends to be much smaller than the state contribution.

The federal government spent just under $70 billion on education in 2015, a tiny fraction of the overall federal budget of $3.8 trillion. By contrast, education spending constitutes about 50 percent of states' overall spending (Figure 3.2). Every other expenditure at the state level is dwarfed by the dollars that go to education. Thus, significant changes to a state budget—such as an effort to reduce class size—are difficult because the range of options for funding it is limited.

WWPT? Would you cut different areas of education programming? Take from the much smaller coffers allocated to other issues like public safety? Or raise taxes?

State and the federal governments give out two types of grants. The first, **categorical** (or block) grants, are given based on formulas that take into account the number of students in a given area and other factors, such as their level of need. Title I federal funding to address equity for low-income students is distributed in categorical grants. The second type of grants are **competitive** grants, which require states, districts, and partners to demonstrate the soundness of their plan and the human capacity to execute that plan in order to be awarded the grant.

The deceptive part about the federal role is this: although the feds contribute a fairly small percentage of dollars to overall education spending, they have the power to leverage the way states and districts spend their dollars. As an example, take the $4.35 billion Race to the Top program that the US Department of Education (ED) launched as part of the American Recovery and Reinvestment Act (Obama's stimulus package after the 2008 financial crash). Race to the Top promised big money, up to $700 million, to states, but only if states oriented their policymaking to policies that ED judged to be good for improving schools. A reported thirty-two states changed state laws—mandating teacher evaluations, expanding access to charter schools, and adopting higher standards—to have access to the federal pot of money.[6]

Figure 3.2 State Spending on Education versus Federal Discretionary Spending, 2015 Data from "Federal Spending: Where Does the Money Go," National Priorities Project, https://www .nationalpriorities.org/budget-basics/federal-budget-101/spending/

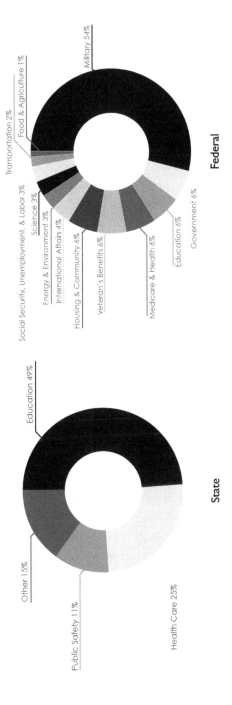

> WWPT? To show my value before I'm up for reelection again, how can I help my constituents secure competitive federal dollars?

Per-pupil spending is another means of mapping persistent patterns of inequity in American education. Average per-pupil spending in America in 2013 (the most recent year for which data are available) was $10,700. However, average spending in New York State, at $19,818, was more than three times higher than in Utah ($6,555). Even within states, there is staggering variation from one district to the next. NPR conducted an investigation of school funding in 2016. It profiled Rondout District 72, spending $28,639 per pupil in an affluent community, in contrast to the Chicago Ridge School District an hour away, which served a mostly low-income community on $9,794 per student.[7]

How Did the Modern Era of Ed Reform Start?

The modern era of education reform as we know it began in 1982 with the release of *A Nation at Risk,* a national report commissioned by the Reagan administration that issued a severe wake-up call regarding our education system.[8] It made clear that our international competitiveness was slipping and that dramatic action needed to be taken to get schools across America back on the right track. The report was the catalyst for the standards and accountability era that continues to this day.

A Nation at Risk led many states to begin—for the first time—crafting standards for what students should know and be able to do at each grade level and in each subject. These were created state by state, with fifty different sets of expectations.

The report also identified the need for a professional teaching force and judged the United States to be falling short on providing top teachers to students. Many of the ideas still being debated today, such as career ladders, higher standards in teacher preparation programs, and rigorous teacher evaluation tied to "salary, promotion, tenure and retention decisions," were first proposed in the report.

> WWPT? If teachers play an important role in improving schools, how can we measure teacher performance and ensure excellent teachers for every student?

Through most of the 1990s, states began implementing their standards and moved into developing assessments to determine whether students were achieving those standards on pace. Even by the mid-1990s when I started teaching (just before state testing began in Massachusetts), it was common for teachers to treat the standards as optional, resulting in students learning some topics over and over and having major gaps in knowledge because other concepts were never taught. For example, when I decided to do a baking soda volcano with my sixth-grade science class, the group oohed and ahhed and then started volunteering, "I did that in second and fourth grade," "I did that last year," "I've done that three times before." We teachers taught what was interesting and what we thought we could teach well. We also set expectations for pace, meaning that kids in different classrooms lived with widely varying expectations as to what was, for example, "third-grade work."

> WWPT? Under what conditions will teachers embrace the new standards?

Twenty-First-Century Ed Reform

The following brief walk-through of the history of the past thirty-five years helps to explain how we landed at a place where annual testing, evaluating teacher performance, and the Common Core State Standards are the most contested issues of the day.

No Child Left Behind

The No Child Left Behind Act of 2001 (NCLB) was the next stage in the evolution of the standards and accountability era of schooling. Its hallmark expectations—annual student testing in grades 3–8 plus high school, and every student reaching grade-level proficiency by 2014 (six years after Bush was safely out of office!)—have been a frustration to most teachers. Judging absolute proficiency on tests rather than on whether students were growing from year to year was unfair to students who started far below grade level (and the teachers working with them). Annual summative tests required by the federal government led to a proliferation of formative and benchmark tests to help prepare kids for the tests at the end of the year, especially in areas where kids weren't doing well, and the consequences for failure were high. Undoubtedly, there were many things about NCLB that ended up being counterproductive to the goal of helping struggling schools improve.

However, if you care about education as a civil rights issue, NCLB elevated our ability to focus on achievement gaps. Annual testing—and the related requirement that data be reported broken out by subgroups like race and poverty level—produced information on the size and scope of achievement gaps that was previously unavailable. You can't fix something you can't see. The intent of annual testing is the same as an annual checkup at the doctor. If testing occurs only every few years, it's too late to catch problems that may have metastasized over a long period. Annual testing allowed us to have more specific conversations about where students were falling behind and what to do about it. Although this has led to some over-reaching efforts to hold teachers accountable, it is a good thing that we know which kids have basic literacy skills by grade 3. The alternative universe of testing only every few years and then asking "Where did we go wrong?" would be worse.

Those of us teaching in the 1990s (and before) could and did just bury our heads in the sand and assume that all kids were getting access to the same high expectations and chance for future success. They weren't. Although we haven't done enough to close achievement gaps in the past couple of decades, keeping them front and center in our collective consciousness is important and can only happen with annual testing.

Today, parents have better information to fight for better schools. District and state leaders know which schools need targeted resources and assistance. This is a good thing, and addressing these issues is the right role for policy. Now, with the Every Student Succeeds Act, there is an opportunity to right-size assessments without losing adult accountability to our neediest students.

NCLB required states to judge student proficiency by grade level in math and literacy, but (in keeping with the American tradition of states' rights) allowed states to establish their own definitions of proficiency. As states began reporting student proficiency on state tests, two issues came to the surface.

1. Our standards for proficiency were generally pretty low relative to other industrialized nations.

2. States set very different bars for what constituted proficiency. States with rigorous expectations for what constituted proficiency (such as Massachusetts) had a relatively small number of students reaching the bar, whereas states that set much lower standards (like Alabama) had a far greater percentage of students "achieving proficiency."

When students from all states took the same test—the National Assessment of Educational Progress (NAEP)—states like Massachusetts were near the top even though the level of student proficiency they were reporting on their own state tests (with cut scores set by state officials) was low. In contrast, Alabama was scoring near the bottom on the NAEP, but reporting high levels of proficiency on their state tests (with cut scores set by their state officials).

> WWPT? Short of a federal mandate, is it possible for states to work together to develop a shared definition of student proficiency at each grade level?

This provoked an important conversation about what it means to prepare students across America to be college and career ready in the twenty-first century. The logic, to many, was simple: students would be competing with their peers across the globe for jobs in the knowledge economy, rather than with their peers in the same town for manufacturing jobs, and our standards needed to reflect that. You don't need to be a psychic to guess what comes next. Enter conversation about common standards across states. Why should students in Alabama be handicapped with lower expectations that make it more difficult for them to compete for college placement and future jobs with students from Massachusetts or Singapore or Korea?

The Common Core

Starting about 2009, a large coalition of state leaders, policy organizations, and philanthropic supporters set out to develop the Common Core State Standards (CCSS), new standards that could be voluntarily adopted by states.[9] (States' rights at work again!) It is important to note that the CCSS were never an initiative of the federal government, although the feds did nudge states toward adopting higher "college and career ready standards" to score well in competitive grant offerings like Race to the Top.

The standards rolled out without too much controversy, until new tests, aligned to the CCSS, got close to coming online and adding accountability for performance. The Partnership for Assessment of Readiness for College and Careers (PARCC) and the Smarter Balanced assessments were developed by cross-state coalitions and teams of experts to create alignment between what students were learning in the Common Core era and what was being assessed. This was a fine idea on its own, but it collided with other reforms like test-based teacher evaluation to create the perfect storm of controversy around testing that continues today—and will be discussed much more in the pages of this book.

Non-Sellout Strategy for Ensuring That Reforms Are Implemented in Ways That Work for Teachers and Students

In a situation many can relate to, teachers Laura Meilli and Alex Seeskin were frustrated that their district had handed down a mandate—implement the CCSS—without any support or professional learning opportunities to help the process. Although their district (the Chicago Public Schools) and union (the Chicago Teachers Union) were in a stalemate that would ultimately lead to a strike just months later, the teachers approached both entities about the need for better professional development on the CCSS. The teachers developed an idea for a conference that would bring other teachers together to share best practices. Though the district CEO and the union president did not jointly work on any other initiatives that year, they both agreed to fund and participate in the teacher-led conference; they even appeared on stage together for the only time that year.

This is a great story of teachers' ability to break through a political impasse to get their leaders to act on behalf of students. It is also a powerful story of the role teachers can play in galvanizing their peers.

As Laura recalls, "We thought we could get two hundred teachers. Wouldn't it be great if two hundred teachers showed up?" More than sixteen hundred teachers showed up. On a Saturday. In July. Teachers from around the country wanted to copy the format. In a single year, teacher-led CCSS conferences spread to each of the Teach Plus sites, reaching nearly five thousand teachers. When registration opened for our Los Angeles conference, more than seventeen hundred teachers signed up in the first twenty-four hours—an unprecedented show of demand for teacher leadership on the CCSS.

At the time of this writing, the education reform movement is at an inflection point. The past decade's prioritization of teacher quality and accountability is giving way to increased focus on race, poverty, and how the world outside the classroom affects students' opportunities to learn. The past, present, and future of US education each have (or will have) its own unique call for "reform." The system is a work in progress that is difficult to summarize or evaluate comprehensively.

There Are Lots of Ways to Tell the Story of How Good or Bad US Education Is

Advocacy for any new or continued policy is essentially case making. In our decentralized system, education is a messy mix of programs layered on top of one another in schools. It is very difficult to accurately identify a causal relationship between any one component of a student's school experience and its outcome on the student's learning. There is no correct answer to the question of whether American schools are "good enough." That question simply serves to frame the basic debate about what direction education policy should take.

Because there is no single answer to whether schools are good or bad, political actors tend to choose the narrative that aligns to their cause. Anticipating cuts to school funding and showing a basic distrust of government institutions like education, President Trump in his inaugural address characterized schools as "flush with cash" but "failing students." By contrast, Hilary Clinton's position was that schools are good and could be better with more funding: "How about funding special education which we never have to the extent we promised? How about fully funding whatever we ask the local communities to do?"[10] Both of these assertions have supporters in broad swaths of the American populace.

There are legitimate large-scale trends which suggest that many of the reforms of the last decade or more are having the desired effect. Achievement gaps—particularly between African American and White students—have narrowed. African American students on average have gained two full grade levels on the NAEP tests and one full grade in ELA. Graduation rates are up significantly for all student groups and the most for African American and Hispanic students. Locations like Tennessee and the District of Columbia, which have moved aggressively toward improving teacher quality, have seen the greatest gains on the NAEP tests. These data, tracked across millions of students, are meaningful and positive.[11]

At the same time, our competitiveness on international exams such as the Program for International Student Assessment (PISA) tells a different story. American students perform in the middle of the pack among sixty-four participating nations in both science and math, though math scores are improving, with younger students doing better than high schoolers. And even though achievement gaps may be narrowing, they still exist at every grade level and in all tested subjects.

The rhetoric dividing "reformers" and "traditionalists" is more polarized than it has ever been. Some of the differences are rooted in beliefs about local control, states' rights, and the role of the federal government in setting and holding states accountable for meeting standards. For example, you should now be able to see how the history of our system influences leaders on either side of the political aisle to form differing baseline opinions of the CCSS, opinions that have nothing to do with how it is being implemented in schools or whether it is helping students learn better.

Political ideology drives these conversations at least as much as beliefs about what is working for kids.

Finally, policy discourse is awash in silver-bullet fixes. These fixes are all a mismatch for our decentralized education system serving a wildly diverse population in terms of income level and race. Every policymaker and his mom has gone on a junket to Finland and come back reporting that if we just treated teachers as professionals and stopped testing kids (as in Finland), we'd be first in the world. Beware comparisons to a single centralized system in a socialist nation with a homogenous population in terms of race and income that is one sixty-fourth the size of the United States.

This is not a book about analyzing whether US education is great or in dire straits. This is a book about preparing you to be effective in policy conversations. To be effective, you need to recognize that you'll encounter people who hold a wide range of opinions about how troubled schools are. Listen for their underlying beliefs. Those beliefs will affect how motivated they will be to take action and why. Be prepared to share your own point of view and back it up, not just with data from your classroom but from around the country and world.

Key Takeaways

☐ The majority of K–12 students today are students of color, a population that our system has never served well.

☐ The 3.1 million teachers serving fifty million students make up only about half of the employees of school districts.

☐ The majority of teachers now have less than ten years' experience, and they vary in significant ways from their predecessors.

☐ In the decentralized US education system, almost 90 percent of funding comes from states and localities, evidence of a strong tradition of states' rights and local control of schools. The federal role has historically been limited, but has grown of late.

☐ Current debates over policy issues like testing and the CCSS have their origins in the standards and accountability movement that came out of the landmark report *A Nation at Risk.*

☐ There is no right or wrong answer to the question of whether schools are "good enough." Thus opinions and evidence on either side of the debate frame policy decision making.

Notes

1. "Fast Facts: Back to School Statistics," National Center for Education Statistics (2016), https://nces.ed.gov/fastfacts/display.asp?id=372.
2. Ibid.
3. "Fast Facts: Charter Schools," National Center for Education Statistics (2016), https://nces.ed.gov/fastfacts/display.asp?id=30.
4. "Number and Percentage Distribution of Teachers in Public and Private Elementary and Secondary Schools, by Selected Teacher Characteristics: Selected Years, 1987–88 through 2011–12" (Table 209.10), National Center for Education Statistics (July 2013), https://nces.ed.gov/programs/digest/d13/tables/dt13_209.10.asp.
5. Greg Toppo, "GAO Study: Segregation Worsening in US Schools," *USA Today,* May 17, 2016, http://www.usatoday.com/story/news/2016/05/17/gao-study-segregation-worsening-us-schools/84508438/.
6. National Council on Teacher Quality, *State of the States: Trends and Early Lessons on Teacher Evaluation and Effectiveness Policies* (October 2011), http://www.ewa.org/sites/main/files/nctq_stateofthestates.pdf
7. "Why America's Schools Have a Money Problem," *School Money,* National Public Radio (April 17, 2016), http://www.npr.org/series/473636949/schoolmoney.
8. National Commission on Excellence in Education, *A Nation at Risk: The Imperative for Educational Reform* (April 1983), https://www2.ed.gov/pubs/NatAtRisk/risk.html.
9. Common Core State Standards Initiative, "Development Process" (n.d.), http://www.corestandards.org/about-the-standards/development-process/.
10. "Hillary Clinton on Education: Hillary Clinton on Education Funding," *On the Issues,* http://www.ontheissues.org/2016/Hillary_Clinton_Education.htm#Education_Funding.
11. "The 74 Debate: Huffman vs. Barnum on Duncan's Legacy, Testing Backlash and the Future of Reform," *The 74* (January 5, 2016), https://www.the74million.org/article/the-74-debate-huffman-vs-barnum-on-duncans-legacy-testing-backlash-and-the-future-of-reform.

CHAPTER · FOUR
Language

LESSON
Bilingualism Is the Price of Admission to Decision Making

My daughters all started full-day French immersion in their public school in first grade, and now as eighth, sixth, and fourth graders, they are fully bilingual (at least enough to talk about my husband and me to each other behind our backs). Their parents' monolingualism is the source of lots of teasing in our house. Because I took a few years of French in high school, they like to have me try to translate short passages with words they think should be easy. I can usually get most of the gist, but the nuance that I miss and the (rare!) words I completely botch inevitably send them into peals of laughter.

They would find it ironic that in my work life, I see my purpose as helping others become bilingual. I recognize that both of the languages I'm translating are English, but the analogy holds. Teachers and policymakers use some of the same words, but because those words have completely different background contexts, many points get lost in translation. The language of the classroom—that is, the language of practice—has one vocabulary, one set of guiding assumptions and goals. The language of elected officials and government leaders—that is, the language of policy—has an entirely separate vocabulary and set of assumptions and goals.

Take a simple term like *class size*. When a teacher talks to anyone about class size, she is thinking about actual human beings, sometimes more than there are desks in her room, staring her in the face expecting a graded essay and a sympathetic ear if it's that kind of day. When a policymaker talks about class size, she is thinking about a major budget driver and a set of related cost implications. It is possible for a teacher to have an effective conversation with a policymaker about class size, but not without knowing the thought bubble that enters the policymaker's brain when the term is raised.

This chapter lays out a framework that delineates the differences between the language of policy and the language of practice. This framework is summarized in Table 4.1.

Knowledge Base

Think back for a moment to your teacher preparation program and the courses you took. Then think back to that room full of policy people whom I introduced at the start of chapter 2, the people who stump most teachers

Table 4.1 Sources of the Gap between Policy and Practice

Dimension	Practice	Policy
Knowledge Base	Subject-matter content Classroom management Child and adolescent development Research on classroom practice (sometimes)	Legal and financial rules governing education Procedure for initiating and leading policy change Power dynamics of groups Research on systems (sometimes)
Locus of Control: Focal Unit	Individual and class	District, state, nation
Locus of Control: Unit Size	Approximately 1–100	Approximately 1,000–50 million
Type of Influence	Direct	Indirect
View of Education Process	Focused on inputs	Focused on outcomes
Primary Levers for Change	Relationships with students, parents, other teachers, principals	Legislation, regulation, budgets, contracts
Key Marker of Personal Success	Impacting the life of a child	Reelection or reappointment
Major Pressures of the Job	Individual students Time scarcity Factors outside of school	Equity Resource scarcity Accountability

as to what they are doing all day. One way of understanding who they are is to figure out what types of knowledge they have. Although there are plenty of people with JDs or MBAs in the room, let's compare the ones who might have been in an ed school at the same time you were earning your teaching license.

Vanderbilt is one of the top education schools in the country, and it lists its course requirements very clearly online. Table 4.2 offers a side-by-side comparison of the different types of expertise one can have in education.

The two individuals who emerge from these two respective programs may share a healthy dose of Vandy Pride, but that's about all. There is

Table 4.2 Nonoverlapping Disciplines

Elementary Masters Degree + Licensure Program[1]	Policy Masters and PhD Programs[2]
Curriculum and Instructional Design	Politics of Education
Theory and Practice of Literacy Education (2 courses)	Sociology of Education
Theory and Practice of Writing in Elementary Grades	Economics of Education
Teaching Literacy for Diverse Learners	Research Design and Methods
Mathematical Concepts for Elementary Teachers (2 courses)	Intro to Statistics (Inference)
Science Concepts for Elementary Teachers (2 courses)	Regression Analysis I
Advanced Teaching of Social Studies in Elementary Schools	Regression Analysis II
Principles of ELL Education	Causal Analysis
Psychological Foundations of Education	Qualitative Research Methods
Educational Psychology of Exceptional Learners	Research Design and Data Analysis
Classroom Organization and Management	Politics and Policy Making

literally not a single point of overlap in their coursework. They come out with different types of knowledge, skills, mind-sets, and ways of analyzing the world. The folks on the right side speak the language of policy, and the folks on the left side speak the language of practice.

Teachers know what makes kids tick. They study classroom management and child development, and how to differentiate, challenge a heterogeneous group, and motivate. They develop expertise in one or more subjects based on the grade level they teach. They learn to develop curriculum and pedagogical technique. They may have reviewed research, primarily about what works in the classroom and what doesn't. They are trained to participate in a profession as practitioners in the same way that doctors are given hands-on practice in a classroom as part of their training.

People who earn an advanced degree in policy are trained as social scientists and researchers. I was slightly disheartened to find this out *after* I completed my PhD and went looking for a policy job. I had an interview at a think tank where the founder closed the meeting by saying, "I'd like to offer you a position as director of research."

"Research," I said. "I wasn't really looking for a research position."

"You're a trained researcher," he reminded me. "Those skills are what you have to offer to education policy."

He was right. I chose to do my PhD to become an "education expert." After the fact, I realized that I hadn't become more expert in "everything education." I'd shifted from teaching practice as my primary form of expertise to research on policy.

I had completed over a dozen courses in statistics and research methods and economics. My brain had gone through a complete immersion in the legislative process and how to analyze large data sets. I was trained to design research that could later meet the criteria for journal publication and to critique the research of others. I was even further from real kids than I was when I was in my first job out of the classroom at the Department of Education. My vocabulary, mind-set, and way of looking at the world were based on the capital *K* Kids. I was officially an expert in systems thinking.

All the while, I felt the tug of my first love, actual kids in schools. The Talking Heads song was still there in the shower: "How did I get here?" How weird that I wasn't fulfilling my lifelong dream to be teaching. Can you ever go home again? Could I ever blend the two worlds I inhabited?

Eventually, Teach Plus became my way to bridge those worlds. The first day I ever taught our Policy Fellows course to teachers, I knew I'd found my calling—teaching about the subject I most loved, ed policy. But take it from someone who voluntarily submitted to a doctoral program that brainwashed me into becoming a policy researcher: the knowledge base is very different.

I'm a firm believer that teachers shouldn't have to and don't have to leave the classroom to become fluent in policy-speak. There are great resources available and great teachers to follow to build your knowledge.

Non-Sellout Strategy for Becoming a Policy Geek

Here is my list of favorite go-to resources for the teacher who wants to become a policy geek. Remember, my personal approach is to know what your likely allies are thinking, but not to get yourself into an echo chamber. Read up on all sides of an issue.

The Standards
- Read *Education Week* (www.edweek.org) regularly. This was the first piece of advice I was given as I moved from the classroom to the policy world, and it's often still the first piece of advice I give. *Ed Week* has a number of good blogs as well.
- Subscribe to the Teach Plus *NewsBlast* (teachplus.org/news-events/newsletters/subscribe-newsletters). Every week, you'll get the top policy articles of the week, as well as the work of teachers writing on policy issues, and you'll have access to teacher leadership opportunities.
- Sign up for the *Teacher's Edition* (www.ed.gov/teaching/teachers-edition-archive), a US Department of Education newsletter that covers policy, research, and teacher voice.

Teachers to Follow Who Know Their Stuff on Policy
- Marilyn Rhames (@MarilynRhames) (http://educationpost.org/network/marilyn-rhames/)
- Jon Alfuth (@jwalnuth)
- Maddie Fennell (@maddief)
- National Network of State Teachers of the Year (NNSTOY) has a weekly newsletter with contributions from current and former teachers (@NNSTOY)

Blogs I Read
- Andy Rotherham (www.eduwonk.com) (@arotherham)
- Real Clear Politics (www.realclearpolitics.com)

(*continued*)

- Justin Cohen (www.justinccohen.com) (@juscohen)
- TNTP (tntp.org/blog)

Policy Shops That Lean Left
- Learning Policy Institute (learningpolicyinstitute.org)
- Center for Teaching Quality (www.teachingquality.org)

Policy Shops That Lean Right
- Fordham Institute (edexcellence.net)
- AEI (www.aei.org/policy/education)

Locus of Control

I still remember the sinking feeling of knowing which students in my classes I couldn't seem to relate to well enough. *Joey V, I know you are trying to be invisible to me, and I know I am not doing enough to stop you from being invisible to me. I know our lack of a personal connection is a negative for your learning.* The faces of individual students would pop into my head throughout the day and night, accompanied by thoughts about what more I could be doing for that kid. That is the world of a teacher: highly personal, with very direct influence over a relatively small group of individuals. (Those of you who are teachers with crazy class sizes over 125 may dispute the "small group" reference, but hang with me for the next couple of paragraphs.)

Whereas teachers spend a full year (often more) with the same group of 25 to 125 individuals and then continue relationships with them in the same school for years to come, policymakers have a completely different locus of control. The unit size of the population they serve might range from a couple thousand students in a district to fifty million students for those working at the federal level. The **direct** influence on kids that is the hallmark of the work of teaching is replaced by **indirect** influence over a much larger group. Instead of being charged with the progress of a class, policymakers are charged with the progress of a system.

It is literally impossible for policymakers to know all or even most of the people who are affected by their decision making. (Recall the earlier point that all policy is made in an environment of imperfect information.) In essence, having a thousand kids in your charge is more similar to having ten million than it is to having a hundred. Once you hit a certain number, you are in the realm of capital K abstract Kids. Likewise, it is much harder to feel your impact on Kids. Policy begins where individual relationships end.

Policy begins where individual relationships end.

For the most part, policy is gray because its effects are indirect. Maybe the policy I was involved with was having an impact, maybe it wasn't. In most cases, it was hard to tell from my office, which was a mile away from the closest school (that I had never even visited). What I know is that I have never been as clear about how much my own work mattered as when I had direct control over my own classroom.

View of the Education Process

What teachers see of the education process are the daily human interactions they have with students. They can answer the question, "What are you doing each day to educate students?" Their view is on the **inputs** in the education system. Time spent with kids, which curricula are used, and whether supplementary supports are available are all inputs into the education process. By contrast, policymakers tend to focus on **outcomes**. They need to answer the question, "What are the results that schools are producing, and are they better than in the past?" They have greater access to large data sets on student achievement or on teacher evaluation ratings and see their responsibility as ensuring that the system is producing the best possible outcomes.

Primary Levers for Change

Take a look at the following quotations from transcripts of real speeches that I use when I teach about bilingualism and the stark language differences between teachers and policymakers. You'll recognize one name immediately: President Obama. The second is Pearl Arredondo. She is an amazing teacher in Los Angeles who was part of our policy fellows program; through that program, she got invited to do a TED Talk at an event where John Legend and Bill Gates were two of the other speakers.

Here at Graham Road, they're using innovative approaches to provide effective teaching to all their students and that's something that all of America's schools have to do. As I said before, there are any number of actions we can take as a nation to enhance our competitiveness and secure a better future for our people, but few of them will make as much of a difference as improving the way we educate our sons and daughters. Offering our children an outstanding education is one of our most fundamental—perhaps our most fundamental—obligation as a country. And whether we meet that obligation not only reflects who we are as Americans; it will shape our future as a nation. Countries that out-educate us today will out-compete us tomorrow, and I refuse to let that happen on my watch. Now, it's clear that doing the same old things will not get the job done for our kids, or for America, or for our future. So when I took office, I asked Arne Duncan to work with states and local school districts to take on business as usual in our education system, and that's how the Race to the Top competition was born last July. It's a national competition among states to improve our schools. Over the past few months, we've seen such a positive response that today I'm announcing our intention to make a major new investment, more than 1.3 billion dollars in this year's budget to continue the Race to the Top.

—*President Obama*[3]

So, I grew up in East Los Angeles not even realizing I was poor. My dad was a high-ranking gang member who ran the streets. Everyone knew who I was, so I thought that I was a pretty big deal and I was protected. And even though my dad spent most of my life in and out of jail, I had an amazing mom who was just fiercely independent. She worked at the local high school as a secretary in the dean's office, so she got to see all the kids that got thrown out of class for whatever reason who were waiting to be disciplined. Man, her office was packed! So see, kids like us, we have a lot of things to deal with outside of school, and sometimes we're just not ready to focus, but that doesn't mean that we can't; it just takes a little bit more. Like, I remember one day I found my dad convulsing, foaming at the mouth, OD'ing on the bathroom floor. Really?

Do you think that doing my homework that night was on the top of my priority list? Not so much, but I really needed a support network. A group of people who were going to help me make sure that I wasn't going to be a victim of my own circumstance. That they were going to push me beyond what I even thought I could do. I needed teachers.

—Pearl Arredondo[4]

I love these talks because they are such perfect illustrations of the language differences that make communication across levels difficult. Look them up online and you'll see that everything about their respective styles is different as well. Obama, of course, is wearing a suit, speaking in a speech-y, starched, my-talk-was-reviewed-by-a-dozen-wonks way. Pearl is wearing slightly dressy teacher clothes. As she moves across the stage telling her personal story, it is easy to picture her owning her classroom this way every day.

Obama is focused on "international competitiveness" and the theoretical obligation all Americans have to ensuring a strong education system for future generations. Pearl is focused on "kids like me" and what's happening outside school that matters to kids. Sure, Pearl could give you a definition of international competitiveness, but is that what motivates her? Is there much about America's overall international competitiveness that is in her control?

Obama talks about the need for "innovation in every school" in his first sentence and goes on to say, "it's clear that doing the same old things will not get the job done." From there, he announces his new and improved solution, the Race to the Top competitive grant program. Obama is painting a picture of a rapidly changing world and schools that need a catalytic push (from government) to catch up.

From Pearl, in stark contrast, you'd be more likely to come away with an impression that the biggest challenges schools face are timeless—how to help kids to learn when the world outside the classroom is bigger and more interesting and always pushing into school. Whereas Obama argues that "doing the same old things will not get the job done," Pearl would be likely to disagree if "the same old things" include teachers building strong personal relationships with kids.

They're both talking about schools and kids, so why are their language and perspective so different?

Simply put, Pearl is talking about the world she sees and has some control over, and Obama is doing the same.

Let's assume they both care about giving kids a good education. What can Pearl do if she wants to be successful on that front? The levers most immediately at her disposal operate at the individual level. She can stay after school with students. She can work with other teachers to strategize different approaches. She can build a connection to parents. She can work with administrators in her school to adjust the schedule or make other accommodations. Her levers for making a difference are individual and relationship based.

What about an elected official? Sure, he can have single drive-by meetings with individuals whose stories of underresourced schools are the inspiration and moral compass behind a policy action. I think about the president tearing up when he announced his executive action on gun control, referencing the families he'd met from Sandy Hook. He was inspired by real people who'd lost their children. However, he cannot be there on a daily basis to help in the healing process the way teachers can. He can only help set the conditions to limit the likelihood that something like that will happen in another school.

Policymakers have a completely different set of levers at their disposal, ones that affect the entire system. The levers they can pull include allocating resources differently than in the past, enacting new laws, or enforcing new regulations. At a district level, changes to the teachers' contract are a key lever for changing policy. A policymaker may be inspired to action by the story of one student, but the tools available to that person move systems.

Pearl's view into how schools are succeeding (and not) is reflected in the faces of actual kids from whom she cannot turn away because she sees them day after day. Her first line of defense in changing things for them lies right there in the people in her school. Obama's view of how schools are doing is reflected in large data sets, stories from the largest districts in the country, and national movements, like the opt-out movement, that make it into the national media. His role (and only option) is to change laws or set new regulations (for example, regulation to limit testing) and then leave it to schools like Pearl's to (we hope) implement the new rules.

Key Markers of Personal Success

For teachers, feedback on how they're doing at their job is direct and frequent. They can read it in the faces of the kids in their classroom on a minute-to-minute basis. Almost twenty years later, I can still easily recall how I felt and the specifics of what I was doing when I really knew I was knocking it out of the park as a teacher (teaching about the world map as it was changing in real time). I can recall, just as specifically, my big flops (an unannounced observation the day after my twenty-third birthday that involved a Jeopardy!-themed test review gone awry). The experience of directly impacting students' lives leaves an indelible impression. That is the key marker of success for a teacher.

Policymakers don't experience that immediate personal moment by which to judge their success as they are taking action. The moment is rarely "live" and packed with emotion the way it is when a struggling kid finally "gets it."

For a policymaker, personal success plays out at the system level. It might be corralling enough votes in the legislature to pass a new law or securing a majority on the school board to ensure that a new program is adopted. It might be getting reelected or reappointed to the position as a decision maker, indicating that others believe he or she has been a good steward of the public interest.

Recall the speech by President Obama from earlier in the chapter. It was given in January 2010 as he was preparing for the first round of feedback on what voters thought of how he and his party were doing—the 2010 congressional elections. He was using the levers he had at his disposal: federal funds for a nationwide competition to improve schools. But his approach also illustrates the incentives that get created when your success is defined by something

> The incentives of policymakers to introduce new initiatives to demonstrate their worth are pretty much directly at odds with most teachers' interest in not having to implement new policies year after year.

indirect, such as reelection. An inescapable element of getting reelected is demonstrating to constituents that improvements are being made under your leadership. Would the president be able to claim such improvements definitively if he took the approach Pearl might suggest: leaving schools free of new expectations and programs, free to make decisions about how to spend time with students? Heck no. No new policy initiatives, no visibility for the elected official as a leader on improvement in schools.

The incentives of policymakers to introduce new initiatives to demonstrate their worth are pretty much directly at odds with most teachers' interest in not having to implement new policies year after year.

Major Pressures of the Job

Another way of thinking about the differences between the work of policy-making and the work of teaching is to ask the question, What are the key pressures that you face in your job? In other words, what keeps you up at night? What must you be responsive to, or else you *cannot* be successful in your work? I've asked this question in group conversations with close to a thousand teachers in our policy fellows program. State and district officials are monthly guests in those policy fellows sessions, and I like to ask the same question of them in front of teachers.

Teachers have one North Star in terms of concerns: their **individual students**. Whether worrying that the state test is going to be demoralizing for their English language learner, or puzzling over how to care for the eighth grader experiencing trauma at home—regardless of the particular issue on a given day, the fine-grain characteristics of the lives of "our kids" create an inescapable pressure, even if it is one that teachers are putting on themselves.

Time scarcity is a second omnipresent pressure in the lives of teachers everywhere. The needs of each individual student are vitally important, but attempting to meet those needs is jammed in with other requirements of the job—prepping for classes, grading, mandatory meetings, and the continual parade of tests and bureaucratic forms. I have never been in a group of teachers who did not lead with time scarcity as the impossibility of their job.

Figure 4.1 The Playing Field of Teaching Practice

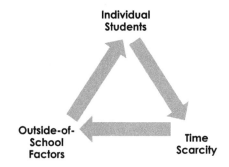

Finally, as Pearl argued so compellingly, kids (and teachers) have a big **life outside of school**, and that outside pressure impacts a teacher's ability to help children learn. A math lesson on converting decimals to fractions may be competing with a growling stomach that hasn't had food since last night. Outside pressure may come in the form of a threatened school closure because test scores are low. There are lots of factors outside teachers' control that affect their ability to be successful, especially when success is narrowly defined by a single test in ELA and math. (Teachers often add pressures of their own, which result from the choice to be a teacher. *Will I have a job next year because I lack seniority and there is going to be a staff reduction in my district? Will I be able to stay in teaching* and *afford to buy a home?*)

These three fundamental pressures—individual students, time scarcity, and outside factors—interact with one another to make the job of teaching incredibly challenging. If you could remove just one from the equation— time pressure, say—the other two might be easier to surmount. But the three bind together and form a triangle that we'll call the playing field of teaching practice (Figure 4.1). These are defining features that make the job what it is. Sure, it would be easier to succeed on a baseball playing field if there were no outfield and a home run were defined as hitting the ball past the bases. The game is hard because to hit a home run, a player needs to make contact with a 90 mph fastball AND hit it four hundred feet AND keep it inside the foul poles.

Like teachers, policymakers have interlocking pressures that make the job what it is. As outlined in Table 4.2, the pressures they cannot ignore boil down to the following:

- **Equity.** Policymakers are charged with setting the conditions for an education system that offers *all* students an opportunity for future success.
- **Resource scarcity.** There are budgetary limitations that necessitate trade-offs among the many services and programs that help students.
- **Accountability.** Given that half of state tax dollars go to fund public education, taxpayers will demand information on whether schools are improving.

Of course, these pressures are compounded by the explicitly political nature of the work and thus the political pressures embedded in the job. Nevertheless, policymakers' playing field is bounded by the three factors (Figure 4.2).

These factors—equity, resource scarcity, and accountability—have very deep roots in the policy process. Because they are so important to understanding the language of policy and what drives policy action, I will spend the next three chapters diving into each one. (Spoiler alert: I'm most passionate about the breakdown in understanding between teachers and policymakers on accountability—nerd heaven to me!)

As a teacher seeking to break down communication barriers and persuade those in decision-making roles, you need to understand policy-

Figure 4.2 The Playing Field of Education Policymaking

makers' playing field. As I shared in chapter 1, most teachers are under the mistaken impression that their role as an advocate is to help policymakers understand the work of a teacher. In fact, teachers need to be doing essentially the opposite. We need to equip legislators to do their job—balancing budgets, assuring constituents that tax dollars are spent wisely, ensuring that resources are distributed equitably across the system. Without our help in answering policymakers' questions in the context of our classroom experience, we are not giving them the ammunition they need to advance our cause.

Non-Sellout Strategy for Ensuring That Your Story Doesn't Get Lost in Translation

The following story is an amalgam of a few different experiences I've had. It is meant to illustrate how easily a conversation between a policymaker and teacher can get lost in translation.

Let's say you're a math teacher who gets a meeting with your state representative to weigh in on a pending decision—whether your state should go back to its old home-grown assessment system or continue after its first year of piloting the PARCC tests. To assert your own credibility, you introduce yourself by sharing that your tenth graders, most of whom are low-income students and nonnative English speakers, have all passed the state test for three years in a row. You've got the legislator interested. Good! He asks how you did it. You share that you started a wildly popular after-school math club. He asks if you're paid to do that. You share that you've figured out how to raise funds for the club by writing grants—a point of pride for you. From there, you talk for more than an hour, and you feel like you've gotten your point across on which test you think is best. Mission accomplished!

A week later, you read in the paper about a completely separate education issue—a pending bill on extending the school day. The most controversial element of it is that teachers would not make as much money in the additional hours as they do during the current school day. Your state representative is quoted in the article saying he has come out in favor of the bill because "he has heard from teachers, and the best ones are already

(continued)

creating after-school programming and are willing to do it for free, even fundraise for it themselves." Oh no! You want to rewind that meeting. That was not what you intended at all.

There is a lot of potential for this type of "loss in translation" as ideas and anecdotes move back and forth between the world of practice and the world of policy. However, if you are clear on what the state representative sees as his job—figuring out how to offer the most education benefit to the most students, with limited funding—you are better equipped to expect a change in direction during the conversation and to avoid potential pitfalls. The legislator is not a bad person; this is a person who received new information that related to a problem he was being asked to solve at the system level.

If you could replay the meeting with better knowledge of his role in mind, you might share the same opening story but shape the narrative a little differently—maybe suggesting that given the program's strong results, perhaps the state should allocate funding to pilot it in other low-income communities; maybe noting that another great teacher stopped running the same program at her school because the time demands of running it and fundraising were too great. Same story, different understanding of audience.

This brings up two principles to always keep in mind in navigating the space between practice and policy.

Unintended Consequences Are Inevitable

Translating a good idea from the individual or small-group level into a policy for a larger group *always* has unintended consequences. Unintended consequences are a fact of life in policy. Policymakers try to anticipate what the negative unintended consequences of a policy might be, but often do not have enough visibility into classrooms to do so. This is another reason teachers should be at the table as policy is being debated.

The process that leads to unintended consequences can grow from a case like the one I've described. The policymaker is inspired by an individual teacher's story. The levers at his disposal to show how impressed he was by the program are the ones that could help expand its reach. He might secure a few million in the state budget for a pilot expansion to three districts.

This budgetary change allows the program to serve more kids. Win! But what he cannot scale is an individual's heroism, expertise, or willingness to commit free time. The unintended consequences might be that several dozen teachers are required to deliver a program for which they have been inadequately trained, resulting in lower morale and possible attrition from the district. Loss.

Many Issues Should Not Be "Solved" at the Policy Level

I often speak with teachers who are having a problem with one aspect of their school life or another and who declare, "This should be a policy throughout the whole district," as in, a longer school day should be district policy, or mentoring for new teachers should be district policy. But *should* it be "district policy"? Think strategically and be careful what you wish for. If one characteristic of policy is that it is always rife with unintended consequences, you'll want to try to determine whether the benefits of a policy will likely outweigh its costs in terms of freedom.

On the topic of a longer school day, for example, maybe one school in the district is currently employing half of their teacher staff to serve after school. Maybe another school is using a nonprofit partner. What are some of the unintended consequences of enforcing the same approach for everyone? Maybe *all* teachers in both schools would be forced to take on longer hours. Maybe other providers would lose their jobs, hurting the local community. Possibilities abound. Before you reflexively wish for ditching our messy, locally controlled world for the "one best" school plan, try to envision the alternate universe. Some issues should be handled at the practice level in schools; a smaller number should be handled with one-size-fits-all policy.

Key Takeaways

☐ Teachers are trained as practitioners, whereas those who study policy are trained as social scientists and researchers. Although they might attend the same ed school, there is no overlap in the skills and knowledge they learn there.

☐ Teachers have direct control over a small unit, whereas policymakers have indirect influence over a large unit, ranging in size from several thousand students to several million.

☐ The levers teachers have for improving education focus on relationships, whereas the levers policymakers have are bureaucratic instruments like budgets, contracts, and legislation.

☐ Personal success in teaching centers on changing the life of a student, whereas the defining mark for a political official is reelection or reappointment.

☐ The pressures that make the work of teaching difficult—that make up the playing field of the job—are different from the pressures faced by policymakers.

☐ All policies that apply to a large group have unintended consequences, so it is important to think through which issues need an overarching policy and which should be left to school-by-school decision making.

Notes

1. Adapted from the Vanderbilt University Peabody College M. Ed. elementary education and teacher licensure requirements (accessed February 25, 2016). The following URL is for the 2017–18 school year: http://peabody .vanderbilt.edu/departments/tl/graduate_programs/masters_program_med/ masters_degree_teacher_licensure/elementary_education_teacher_ licensure.php.
2. Adapted from Vanderbilt University Peabody College, "Masters of Public Policy in Education Program of Study" (accessed February 25, 2016), http:// peabody.vanderbilt.edu/docs/pdf/lpo/MPP_POS_1113.pdf.
3. "Pr. Obama Education Reform 'Race to the Top' Competition," *YouTube* (uploaded January 20, 2010), https://www.youtube.com/ watch?v=Dh6-cauZkzo.
4. Pearl Arredondo, "My Story, from Gangland Daughter to Star Teacher," *TED Talks Education* (May 2013), www.ted.com/talks/ pearl_arredondo_my_story_from_gangland_daughter_to_star_teacher.

CHAPTER FIVE

Equity

LESSON
*Equity Is Everything
(and Nothing)*

P ublic education is the central way that we Americans enact our founding principle that "all men [and women] are created equal." A fair public education system that gives all kids a shot at their own Horatio Alger story is deeply baked into our collective DNA. We all know that liberty and the pursuit of happiness require that citizens have the basic knowledge to function as productive members of society.

If that's all true, then creating an equitable education system that gives all kids the same opportunities to learn should be simple, right? As we all know, just the opposite is true. Although most Americans care about equity, it is also the case that every person has a different definition of what equity means in practice. That definition is often biased by an individual's life experiences.

Equity is everything in terms of the purpose of policymaking in public education. The role of policy and policymakers is to look across the *system* and ensure that the *system* is set up so that ALL Kids in the *system* can learn to high standards. But because there are as many definitions of equity as there are people, "equality of opportunity" serves less as a unifying vision for our education goals and more as a topic for debate. In that sense, equity is the generic aspiration of closing the achievement gap and has no concrete meaning to guide action. A generic aspiration is not enough.

So what would you do if you were a policymaker and you wanted to improve how low-income students and students of color were served in school? You might not know which among the possible policy interventions you could try would work best. You certainly know that you don't have enough money to do everything that could help.

To help you think like a policymaker, I'm going to walk through a logic chain on equity that is, in my experience, part of the tacit knowledge that is shared by and taken for granted by policymakers. It is the subtext of conversation among policymakers. It is what is in the back of their minds when they speak to teachers and the public. It guides decision making. In my experience, the way policymakers think about equity is related to the levers they can pull to address equity in their own work. Those levers are different from the levers teachers pull, which frame their view of equity. These differences in perspective account for much of the polarization that exists in our field.

Fair warning: this chapter may frustrate you. Hang with me. Read it in the spirit that we discussed in chapter 1: that people are not in education to do bad things to kids. Teachers, especially those who live with struggling students every day, think of schools in terms of social justice and the entirety of the life of each child. Policymakers are attuned to what they can control—things like how dollars are spent and what the rules are for receiving them. They operate in those terms. Think of this chapter as you would a cultural immersion—say, trying chopsticks during your first trip to Japan. They may not feel quite right, and you can take them or leave them in the end, but your experience is broadened by walking in someone else's shoes.

What's at Stake?

How we define equity is crucial because resources are allocated based on what the decision makers think is most fair, the best compromise in a permanent condition of scarcity. Recall that about 50 percent of state tax dollars go to public education. There are plenty of people who would argue that we should simply take those dollars and divide them by the number of students in the state to finance education. There are probably just as many people who would argue that affluent areas could do just fine with their local tax base and that state dollars should be distributed almost entirely among high-need students. If you picture these two extreme positions as anchor ends of a continuum, every state funding formula falls on some point in between.

Each state has a funding formula that gives more or less weight to factors that may necessitate additional resources. Funding formulas typically take into account such factors as the size of a district's low-income, special education, and English language learner populations. As evidence that states make different trade-offs (there's that word again!), every year the respected think tank the Education Trust ranks states in terms of how much their funding formulas prioritize low-income students and

> **Policymakers' beliefs about equity and how to achieve it show up in budgeting at all levels of the system.**

students of color.[1] Each year, the Education Trust's analysis shows that some states, like Massachusetts, allocate state funding to ensure that high-poverty areas have more to spend than low-poverty areas, whereas other states, like Illinois, have a far less progressive state funding formula, the net result of which is that poor districts, with greater student needs, have fewer dollars to spend per pupil than the affluent districts. Do you know where your state falls?

Federal spending decisions also involve trade-offs. In fact, philosophical differences between the Obama administration and the Republican Congress over equitable resource distribution of Title I dollars almost prevented the passage of the Every Student Succeeds Act, the successor of No Child Left Behind. A version the Republicans were pushing just weeks before the vote had major urban centers losing tens of millions of dollars each, compared to funding under NCLB. In the end, political jockeying restored most of the money to cities and earned the support of key civil rights organizations as a victory for high-need students.

Policymakers' beliefs about equity and how to achieve it show up in budgeting at all levels of the system.

How Are We Doing at Equity Today?

If a picture is worth a thousand words, then the pictures of Detroit schools that flooded the national media in 2016 told America's equity story best.[2] Mold- and roach-infested classrooms, nonfunctioning bathrooms, and an overall horrifying state of disrepair told the story of the have-nots in America. The media attention gave teachers a platform to talk about unheated classrooms in the dead of the Michigan winter and kids getting sick from buildings the government left to rot. These conditions for poor, mostly Black kids are not dissimilar to the conditions of more than a half-century ago that sparked the *Brown v. Board of Education* decision. They are no better than the conditions in the developing world.

Chapter 3 concluded with data that painted a mixed picture of the overall state of US schools. The picture is not mixed when it comes to how well poor students are doing relative to more affluent students. The picture is not mixed when it comes to how Black and Hispanic students are doing relative to their White and Asian peers. On every possible measure worth counting—achievement at every tested grade level,[3] in every state and in every major city,[4] and in both math and ELA;[5] and college attainment and completion[6]—the outcomes of poor students and students of color remain weaker than those of their peers.

When it comes to achieving equity as a goal of public education, there may be some modest progress,[7] but objectively, our nation is very far from reaching the goal.

So the question for the policymaker who sees these data and cares about these data is, What can I do to improve equity of opportunity in schools? From there, a set of additional questions follow, whose answers are a mix of judgment and fact:

- What is in my control?
- What is known (from the research, my constituents, my experience)?
- What is my personal judgment of what is fair and equitable?
- What do my constituents think is fair and equitable?

As you read the remainder of the chapter, keep these questions in mind.

The Chicken and Egg: In-School versus Out-of-School Factors

School is not a child's only experience. Students are in school 180 days of the year, some for less than six hours a day. Most of their lives—the other 185 days and more than two-thirds of each school day—take place outside the classroom.

In an era of increasing global competitiveness (there I go showing my policy wonk side and sounding like President Obama), affluent parents, even those who send their students to public schools, invest in myriad activities and supports to give their kids a leg up, spending thousands of dollars for private lessons and test prep courses that are out of reach for many families.

In 1966, James Coleman released his landmark report *Equality of Educational Opportunity*, which was based on a study of 650,000 students.

It presented evidence that student background and socioeconomic status were the largest drivers of educational attainment. Since that time, there has been an ideological tug-of-war about the role of school as a lever for social justice. The Coleman Report, as it came to be known, painted a dim view of the power of schools to overcome the effects of poverty and race in an unequal society. Yet, the other side of the argument goes, if you had to disproportionately invest in one social service to help kids escape poverty, wouldn't the highest-leverage investment be education?

Since the Coleman Report, and especially over the last decade, US society has developed even greater extremes in terms of income inequality. The job market, especially for less skilled workers, is less stable. There are many, many social services that need greater investment and attention; and, to many of us, it appears that all of those are getting shortchanged in favor of tax breaks for the wealthy and for big business. Poverty is a factor that permeates a student's school experience and is compounded in schools and districts where concentrations of poverty are high.

In short, our limited tax dollars could be used in numerous ways to benefit students.

If poverty is a huge driver of a kid's chance of making it in America, the natural question is, What can be done to ameliorate the negative effects of poverty? This is an important question for any society. However, there are two different aspects to the question, and only one is useful if you are a policymaker. The first aspect has to do with the **absolute value** of an intervention. Do efforts to ensure that students are properly fed help them in school? What about housing initiatives that address homelessness? Health interventions? Parent education programs? In most cases, the answer is yes, there is an absolute value to these supports. Offering social services can help stabilize families in need and increase the likelihood of student engagement at school.

Unfortunately, the job of policymaking is at its essence focused on the question's second aspect: the **relative value** of one intervention over another. Yes, it is possible to allocate funds to education and hunger and housing and health and parental support programming, but the pie is limited. It may be possible to increase the size of the pie through tax increases, but that cannot be a default solution. If a policymaker believes, as many do, that education is *the* best shot a kid has to escape poverty, wouldn't she focus as much funding as possible on education?

Put yourself in the shoes of your state's commissioner of education. What resource decisions are in your control and what aren't? Where would you start? Would you be willing to give up a piece of your budget for the social services line item to grow? What does someone who believes in education as a lever for social justice do tomorrow if we can't solve poverty without education, but we can't give kids a fair education without addressing poverty?

Addressing poverty and improving education are complex issues, and most reasonable people would agree that both need public attention. However, in our noisy, 140-character-sound-bite world, these issues frequently end up becoming opposing concepts in a chicken-and-egg debate. Efforts to hold teachers accountable for student performance have perverted this debate.

Too often, teachers feel as though they are being blamed by policymakers for factors outside their control. The next section explores the genesis of this policy trend and how teachers can play a role in shifting the debate.

How Does Teacher Policy Relate to Addressing Equity?

Many teachers would say that over the past decade or more, policymakers have been fixated with teacher issues to the exclusion of other strategies that could help students. Am I right? There's been a lot of debate on performance-based pay, evaluation reform, and test-based accountability. This spate of policymaking around teacher quality is rife with unintended consequences, but at this point in the book, you should know that policy isn't random. So why is this happening across fifty states? Where does it come from?

The answer begins with an economic reality: "Generally speaking, a school district spends between 80 and 85 percent of its entire budget on salaries and benefits, meaning only 15 to 20 percent remains to address all of the rest of the budget's priorities and needs."[8] If you are a policymaker who wants to improve schools, you are in essence either looking at salaries and benefits as a possible lever or tinkering around the edges of change.

Next, there is a set of maxims that are widely known in the policy world and have been the gospel of education reform over the last decade. These are research-based ideas that track with decision makers' lived experience. They make sense. They also lend themselves to policy intervention. For each, teachers would be unlikely to dispute the premise, but they may dispute the conclusions that policymakers have drawn from them.

Teachers Are the Most Important School-Based Factor in Student Learning

As we entered the twenty-first century, a number of major education research studies reached an important (but commonsense) finding: that the quality of teachers matters more for students than anything else in a school. If you're a teacher, you're probably reading this and saying, "Duh! I went into teaching because I knew teachers matter in kids' lives. Did they really need to research that?"

The significant point about this research—which accounts for the direction policymaking took thereafter—is that it examined the role of teachers not in **absolute** terms but **relative** to other ways of improving schools. Policymakers are not interested in the question, Do teachers matter in student learning? They are interested in the question, Does spending limited education dollars on teacher quality help kids more than spending those dollars in other ways?

As Linda Darling-Hammond wrote in one of the seminal studies of the time, "Teacher quality variables appear to be more strongly related to student achievement than class sizes, overall spending levels, teacher salaries . . ., and such factors as the statewide proportion of staff who are teachers."[9] The takeaway from the research was, in short: make investments that help teachers become better *rather than* in other options like reducing class size and changing curriculum.

So then the question becomes, What policies should be put in place if we know that teachers matter most? This question represents a case study of the gap between policy and practice. Teachers—whose key lever is *individual* relationships—most often would still advocate for a small class as an essential element of quality teaching. Policymakers—who now more than ever see the need for examining and improving the quality of teachers across a *system*—turn toward interventions like evaluation reform.

The unintended consequence of years of headlines asserting "Teachers Matter Most" was that the debate over school improvement underacknowledged the role of outside-of-school factors in student learning.[10] Yes, great teachers matter, and growing more of them is something policymakers can invest in. However, out-of-school factors, like poverty and childhood trauma, have a huge influence on student learning. Unfortunately, these larger system issues are harder for a policymaker—especially an education official—to address with a silver bullet. The policy focus on how much teachers matter—once intended to be a positive for the profession—has often been experienced by practitioners as an overemphasis on the power of teachers to overcome the impact of factors outside the school.

Teacher Quality Varies Widely, Affecting Students' Life Chances

Like the first point, the notion that not all teachers are equally successful with students also falls into the category of controversial common sense. Anyone who has attended school knows this (including policymakers). Any teacher who reflects for a moment on her school can tell you who the stars are and whose classes she worries about sending kids to next year. However, the norm of egalitarianism runs deep in teaching, attributable at least in part to the philosophy of unity that undergirds unionism.[11] Teachers, especially in the past, have seen more harm than good in surfacing differences in performance from classroom to classroom.

Starting in the late 1990s, a large volume of research started to emerge, adding empirical data to the frequent observation that teacher quality varied. This new research also quantified how much the variability among teachers resulted in variability in student learning. I remember my early days out of the classroom working at the Massachusetts Department of Education. The first piece of research I was handed was a 1996 report by Ted Sanders and June Rivers introducing the concept of value-added in education. Using a large data set of over three million test records from Tennessee, the researchers showed that some teachers produced more learning growth in students than others; that is, they added more value to student learning.

Twenty years after this initial research, the concept of measuring the value-add is more contentious than ever; and, as teacher exposure to the notion has grown, so has teacher resistance to it. For one thing, measuring student learning on the basis of a single test is never adequate to capture all of the learning that happens in a classroom. For another, the tests we give are often poor quality and not aligned to the curriculum teachers are expected to teach.

Regardless of the politics and challenges to implementation surrounding value-add, it is a perfect illustration of the type of concept that has natural appeal for policymakers. The line of research started by Sanders and Rivers has grown quite substantially and reinforced a set of key findings that have huge equity implications.

- "Differences in student achievement of 50 percentile points were observed as a result of teacher sequence after three years."[12] In other words: Imagine two students who start third grade at the 50th percentile on a reading assessment. After three years in a row with top-performing teachers, one of those students might be reading at the 75th percentile and getting recommended for sixth-grade honors classes. His peer, who received three of the weakest teachers in a row, would be reading at the 25th percentile and getting recommended for special education classes. (In the research, teachers are sorted by quintile, meaning that a top teacher is a teacher with value-added scores in the top 20 percent of all teachers.)

- "As teacher effectiveness increases, lower achieving students are the first to benefit."[13] Subsequent research has concluded that three consecutive years with a top teacher could close the achievement gap that exists between Black and Latino students and their White and Asian peers.[14]

- A teacher's effectiveness one year is predictive of that same teacher's effectiveness the following year, even if the composition of the student population in his or her class changes.[15]

From a policy perspective, if you care about equality of opportunity for students, it would be unconscionable to ignore the variation in teacher quality.

Variation in Teacher Quality Exacerbates Achievement Gaps

There is a final piece of the puzzle when it comes to answering the question of why policymakers focus on teacher quality policy as a most favored strategy for addressing equity. Simply, the distribution of quality teachers is uneven, and it disadvantages already disadvantaged students. This is an area in which policy intervention could play a role—for example, by shifting incentives (such as supports and pay bumps) for teachers in high-need schools.

The data show that the teaching force in low-income schools, disproportionately serving Black and Latino students, is newer, weaker, and less stable. Consider the data from a 2012 Education Trust–West study, which found that low-income students were more than twice as likely to have a teacher whose "value-added" was in the bottom 25 percent of teachers, in both ELA and math. The disparity was greater when the access of Black and Latino students was compared to that of White students. The study estimated that the learning advantage for students assigned to top teachers (compared to those assigned the weakest teachers) amounted to fourteen weeks of learning in ELA and four weeks in math.[16] Although value-added scores are an imperfect measure of teacher quality, the trend is unmistakable and appalling.

For decades, countless studies have documented that low-income and minority students are more than twice as likely to be assigned to inexperienced teachers, and that students in new teachers' classrooms do not learn as much.[17]

Finally, rates of voluntary teacher attrition from high-poverty schools are roughly 50 percent higher than for low-poverty schools, and in many cases, districts serving poor students lose half of their staff every five years.[18] This staffing churn—for districts that can least afford a "churn tax"—has massive financial costs.[19] Teacher turnover has also been shown to have negative consequences for student achievement.[20]

＞　＞　＞

Pause for a moment and review the three headings of the sections you've just read. If you were in charge of the education system in your state, what actions would you take given this information?

These three themes explain why so much policy activity is focused on teachers. Looking at the roots of policymaker understanding gives us insight into what can be changed and what cannot. For example, given that we all know—from our own experience and the research—that there is variation in teacher quality, it is unlikely that policymakers will give up on encouraging districts to evaluate teacher performance and provide supports accordingly. However, efforts to limit the use of value-added data in evaluation in favor of other measures have been able to gain traction.

There is opportunity for successful advocacy and teacher leadership on issues like teacher evaluation and differentiated pay. However, advocating to halt efforts to evaluate teacher performance is unlikely to succeed, and is more likely to get teachers excluded from the table when future policy is designed. The entry point for effective advocacy is in improving systems that evaluate and support teaching, and ensuring they are fair for both teachers and kids. To reiterate the principle that motivates me: in professions, practitioners solve the key problems of the field. There are still many issues to solve en route to ensuring that all students have access to what matters most—great teachers.

Non-Sellout Strategy for Improving the Distribution of Excellent Teachers

From late 2007 to early 2009, I worked with my first group of policy fellows in Boston. They read some of the research I've outlined in this chapter and identified a core set of issues that they cared about addressing locally. They were stunned by the data on teacher distribution; they also wanted to find ways to retain excellent, experienced teachers by offering them teacher leadership opportunities that allowed them to help other teachers. Ultimately, the fellows wrote a report proposing a cohort-based model of teacher leadership to support change in chronically low-performing schools.

Although in the past there had been some policy efforts to incentivize strong teachers to teach in low-performing schools, they lacked teacher insight into what incentives mattered to teachers. Prior efforts offered money to individual teachers—often attempting to lure suburban teachers into cities—but little else. The model the teachers proposed was a distinctly

(continued)

"teacher-centric" approach to a policy problem. Its core elements were as follows:

- *A cohort model.* The teachers believed that transforming low-performing schools needed to start with a culture shift, and that the shift could only be effected by a group of empowered, experienced teacher leaders working with the principal.
- *Rigorous selection.* The teachers believed that teacher leaders for this program should, in contrast to past policy initiatives, have an urban teaching background. They also defined selection criteria that included being able to demonstrate a track record of improving student outcomes.
- *Ongoing support from a coach* and *additional pay as incentives.* The teachers placed as much emphasis on funding for the teacher leaders' ongoing professional development as they did on increased compensation.
- *Defined responsibility for teacher leaders.* Teacher leaders, typically one per grade level, would lead teams of teachers at their grade level or subject in setting goals for student progress, making instructional changes, and analyzing their results. The teacher leader would take responsibility for student progress across the grade level.

The group's ideas appealed to local policymakers, who were being pushed by the federal government and a new state law to address staffing in low-performing schools.

The teachers' proposal, dubbed the T3 Initiative, was piloted in three schools in Boston for the 2010–2011 school year. Since that time, it has served over eleven thousand students in twenty-six schools in five locations around the country. Almost a thousand teachers have participated in the program, 270 as teacher leaders and 700 as teacher team members.

T3 has spurred unprecedented improvement in most of these schools and has become a proof point for the power of teacher leadership. Last year alone, across three cities in grades K–2, the program had twenty teacher leaders supporting the improved practice of ninety additional teachers serving more than fifteen hundred students. The average growth across this group on the DIBELS assessment was more than double the growth seen, on average, across the other schools in the district.

> , , ,

What does the future hold for addressing equity in education? Although teacher quality will always be at the heart of debates about equity in schools, it appears that the next wave of education reform should bring some relief for teachers who are feeling as though they are under a microscope. The policy community is increasingly acknowledging that a singular focus on either teacher quality *or* the broader social context that includes income and race will not be sufficient. The equity pendulum appears to be swinging away from teachers and toward a broader conception of the issue.

Key Takeaways

☐ Creating equality of opportunity for students to succeed in school is a primary purpose of education policy.

☐ Although equity is central in policy debates (it is everything), each individual defines equity differently (making it nothing, in concrete terms).

☐ Although there are an infinite number of interventions that could support student success and equity in **absolute** terms, policymakers must weigh the **relative** value of interventions.

☐ Education policy debates often become polarized into a chicken-and-egg debate over whether we must first address poverty to improve education or first improve education to address poverty.

☐ Three ideas that most policymakers accept are (1) that teachers are the most important school-based factor in student learning, (2) that teacher quality varies, and (3) that variation in teacher quality further disadvantages poor students and students of color.

Notes

1. Natasha Ushomirsky and David Williams, *Funding Gaps 2015* (Washington, DC: Education Trust, 2015), http://edtrust.org/wp-content/uploads/2014/09/FundingGaps2015_TheEducationTrust1.pdf.
2. Emma Brown, "Rats, Roaches, Mold—Poor Conditions Lead to Sickout, Closure of Most Detroit Schools," *Washington Post,* January 20, 2016, https://www.washingtonpost.com/news/education/wp/2016/01/20/rats-roaches-mold-poor-conditions-leads-to-teacher-sickout-closure-of-most-detroit-schools/?utm_term=.54b9706f8bfc.
3. National Center for Education Statistics, *NAEP 2012: Trends in Academic Progress* (Washington, DC: US Department of Education, 2013), http://nces.ed.gov/nationsreportcard/subject/publications/main2012/pdf/2013456.pdf.
4. Educational Opportunity Monitoring Project, "Racial and Ethnic Achievement Gaps," Center for Education Policy Analysis, Stanford University (n.d.), http://cepa.stanford.edu/educational-opportunity-monitoring-project/achievement-gaps/race/#third.
5. National Center for Education Statistics, *NAEP 2012.*
6. Terris Ross et al., *Higher Education: Gaps in Access and Persistence Study* (Washington, DC: US Department of Education, 2012), https://nces.ed.gov/pubs2012/2012046.pdf.
7. National Center for Education Statistics, *NAEP 2012.*
8. Noelle Ellerson, "School Budgets 101," American Association of School Administrators (n.d.), https://www.aasa.org/uploadedFiles/Policy_and_Advocacy/files/SchoolBudgetBriefFINAL.pdf.
9. Linda Darling-Hammond, "Teacher Quality and Student Achievement: A Review of State Policy Evidence," *Education Policy Analysis Archives 8,* no. 1 (2000).
10. I got my own very public smack-down for not recognizing the importance of out-of-school factors by columnist Valerie Strauss of the *Washington Post.* In the early days of Teach Plus, we had a line on our website calling "teachers the most important factor in student learning." She wrote on her blog about the inaccuracy of that statement. When we added "in-school" to correct the statement and let her know, she wrote a second post on her blog about how she had successfully forced us to change. I would call it an oversight, but she was right that our language was playing into a larger narrative that had positive intentions for teachers, but untenable expectations for teachers of students in poverty.

11. Susan Moore Johnson and Morgaen L. Donaldson, "Overcoming the Obstacles to Leadership," *Educational Leadership 65,* no. 1 (September 2007): 8–13.
12. William Sanders and June Rivers, *Cumulative and Residual Effects of Teachers on Future Student Academic Achievement* (Knoxville: Tennessee Value-Added Research and Assessment Center, 1996).
13. Ibid.
14. Douglas O. Staiger, Robert Gordon, and Thomas J. Kane, *Identifying Effective Teachers Using Performance on the Job* (Washington, DC: Brookings Institution, 2006).
15. Bill and Melinda Gates Foundation, "Measures of Effective Teaching Project Releases Final Research Report" (press release, January 8, 2013), http://www.gatesfoundation.org/media-center/press-releases/2013/01/measures-of-effective-teaching-project-releases-final-research-report.
16. Carrie Hahnel and Orville Jackson, *Learning Denied: The Case for Equitable Access to Effective Teaching in California's Largest School District* (Oakland, CA: The Education Trust–West, 2012), available at https://edtrust.org/resource/learning-denied-the-case-for-equitable-access-to-effective-teaching-in-californias-largest-school-district/.
17. Kati Haycock and Candace Crawford, "Closing the Teacher Quality Gap," *Educational Leadership 65,* no. 7 (April 2008): 14–19.
18. Kayla Gatalica, *Addressing High Quality Teacher Turnover in DC Public Schools: Lessons from Abroad* (Harvard Graduate School of Education thesis, n.d.), http://isites.harvard.edu/fs/docs/icb.topic1203150.files/Panel%203%20-%20Activating%20the%20Greatest%20Power/USA%20DC_High%20Quality%20Teacher%20Turnover.pdf.
19. Thomas Carroll, *Policy Brief: The High Cost of Teacher Turnover* (Washington, DC: National Commission on Teaching and America's Future, 2007).
20. Matthew Ronfeldt, Susanna Loeb, and James Wyckoff, *How Teacher Turnover Harms Student Achievement* (Washington, DC: National Bureau for Economic Research, 2011).

CHAPTER · **SIX**
Resources

LESSON

"Is It Good for Kids?" Is the Wrong Question

Picture yourself as a teacher in the Chicago Public Schools in early 2013. You've just lived through the stress and uncertainty of a strike earlier in the school year. Now your district has proposed closing fifty-three schools, the largest mass school closure in US history.

It is probably easy to put yourself in those shoes, considering that a seemingly endless onslaught of cuts and administrative change proposals continues in districts around the country, especially since the recession of 2008. You'd probably be frustrated, mostly at anonymous people in the central office. Your job would again feel insecure and, mostly, you'd feel protective of students who already experience more instability than they should have to handle.

At the time of the strike and subsequent debates about school closures during the 2012–13 school year, our Teach Plus team was working with a cohort of policy fellows in Chicago. In fact, I was there to launch that cohort on the first day of the strike in 2012—more than half the group arriving with picket signs and wearing red shirts, the remainder straight from a day of teaching in their charter school classrooms. It was a heterogeneous group of teachers on most issues, but when it came to the possible closures, they all had a personal story of whom the closures would hurt. We had teachers whose schools were on the chopping block. Other teachers talked about feeder schools to their own that were on the list—schools that may have been improving, but not fast enough. Others were frustrated by the largely test-based measures that drove closure decisions. They talked about parents and communities that would suffer if the neighborhood lost its only school. Whereas their perspectives on the strike had been mixed, they more uniformly saw the school closures as a blow to students in the areas of the city already most neglected.

It was in that context that we introduced a simulation exercise on resource allocation to the twenty-five Chicago policy fellows in March 2013. The simulation was developed by Education Resource Strategies (ERS), a nonprofit that advises districts on budgeting. We use it to teach the basics of how resources flow in a school system.

The simulation exercise takes a few hours and is broken into rounds. The groups work with true-to-life data on teacher salaries and other operational costs of running a school district. Although the dollar figures in play are based on real costs, the simulation is not based on a specific district.

Teachers work in groups to balance a $308 million budget, which is a typical budget for a district that serves fifty-six thousand students. Of course, this district is smaller than Chicago, but larger than most US districts.

The first round is focused on making decisions about teacher salaries, because they drive about 80 percent of a district's expenses. Small groups work at their tables and set spending priorities based on real calculations of how each option would affect the budget. For example, do they want to prioritize high first-year salaries to attract more candidates to the district? Or do they want to back-load larger raises for experienced teachers to improve retention? Do they want equal raises for all? Or should larger raises go to higher performers? Do they want a teacher career ladder? If so, are they budgeting for stipends? Release periods covered by other staff?

The costs associated with each decision are specified, so it is clear that the participants cannot say yes to every possibility. The teachers discuss the trade-offs associated with the particulars of different models of staffing and, ultimately, commit to a plan.

Almost every time, they learn that even after making lots of hard choices, they have still overspent.

Round two has the groups revisit the choices in their staffing model, and they are given a list of other realistic options for balancing the budget, with associated price tags. Here's their list:

- Reducing premium spending by closing very small schools (those with fewer than 250 students)
- Raising core class sizes by two for grades 10–12
- Raising noncore class sizes by four in secondary schools
- Reducing special education spending by rethinking IEPs and student assignment to optimize expertise and instructional aides
- Reducing facilities and maintenance spending by 10 percent
- Reducing employee benefits spending by 5 percent
- Freezing salary step for one year for all employee contracts

The groups are forced to make difficult decisions and battle through different underlying theories of how to best serve students. Of course, in terms of **absolute value,** funding everything would be beneficial to students. But the exercise is about assessing the **relative value** of doing one thing instead of another in a resource-limited world. It is a stressful and contentious process, even when the stakes are nonexistent.

In the end—because they must—every group balances the budget. In the end, they are willing to defend their choices, but with a clear recognition and heaviness of heart around the fact that their hypothetical policy decision making has clear consequences. Some people and programs would benefit more than others, and that is unavoidable. I wish every teacher could experience this reality of policymaking up close.

Back to Chicago. Take a guess: How many teachers in that room in 2013 chose to close schools in order to balance the budget and preserve decent teacher salaries? If you guessed all of them, you're right.

So, what are the takeaways from this story?

In their individual work, teachers have few opportunities to get a real sense of the trade-offs associated with budgeting, the real cost of different parts of an education budget, and how seemingly disparate financial issues—like teacher raises in fall 2012 and school closures in spring 2013—are related. This contributes to a polarization between administrators and teachers that is de-professionalizing to teachers. It renders teachers ill-equipped to weigh in on decisions that affect their classrooms. Without some understanding of how schools are financed, teachers cannot take greater ownership of the challenges facing their profession.

> Without some understanding of how schools are financed, teachers cannot take greater ownership of the challenges facing their profession.

When teachers are exposed to a (semi)real budgeting process, I've seen two consistent results. First, teachers are capable of balancing the budget and, further, have really compelling reasons for making the choices they make. Often those choices are different from the ones their district is currently making, and their analysis of why they make different choices is fascinating. They feel the burden of letting down some factions within the system. That is typically not a part of their work experience.

Second, this exercise produces more aha moments about the language of policy and its foreignness to the language of practice than anything else we teach. Teachers often leave the room having made choices they would have sworn they would never make when they entered the room operating in an absolute value world. When they are forced to make choices—like the Chicago teachers seeing that school closure might be the lesser among a set of evils—they experience deeper clarity on how the building blocks of a budget relate.[1]

If the question was, Is it good for kids? The answer would be yes to raising teacher salaries. The answer would also be yes to keeping all existing schools open. The answer would be yes to the next twenty supports you might name. But that question isn't a policy question. The policy question is, *Is it a better investment for kids than something else?*

I feel a sense of success when I see former policy fellows posting their district's proposed budget on Facebook as soon as it comes out and telling their peers to take a look. It is possible for teachers to understand much more of the budgeting process than most do today. It is possible to be much more involved by sharing information with colleagues, testifying at school committee meetings and hearings, and raising your voice in the media. Again, knowing the basics is a prerequisite to being taken seriously.

Non-Sellout Strategy for Influencing Resources

I started the chapter with the Chicago example because it highlights how adopting a relative-value mind-set actually changes teachers' perspectives. In that case, the teachers better understood the budget trade-offs associated with the school closure proposal, but that didn't mean they were on the front lines of decision making.

That example begs an important question: Is understanding how resources move through the system a nice thing for teachers to know (BORING!), or can it actually lead to teachers influencing a real budget (EXCITING!)?

I have a second story, this one from Indianapolis, that is a really powerful example of the role teachers can play in the budgeting process. It involved the same ERS simulation process, but this time with over 150 teachers in the room as well as the district superintendent, the union leadership, and many school committee members. The context, as of 2015 when the event took place, was a four-year wage freeze. In 2011, the state legislature passed a law that required teacher pay, in part, to be based on performance. The district and union had been at an impasse on the terms of a new pay structure, and thus pay was stuck—and frustrated teachers were leaving the district in droves.

The simulation forced choices with realistic budget constraints, but did not use the specific budget of Indianapolis. As the groups made their choices, a set of themes emerged. Most people in the room supported the following:

- Increasing starting salaries substantially
- Creating substantial pay incentives for teacher leaders, especially in challenging schools
- Keeping reimbursement for taking higher education courses, but not tying coursework to a pay increase, as it had been in the past
- Deprioritizing the growth of pay for additional years of experience

Several months later, the contract was settled, and each of these elements occupied a prominent place in its compensation model. Starting salaries went from the lowest in the region to among the highest. Teachers could reach the top levels of the salary scale faster, and excellent teachers willing to take on more responsibility could earn stipends of up to $18,000.

What were some of the actions teachers took to influence resource decision making?

1. **They got involved in their unions.** Three teachers who had been through our policy fellowship ran for vice president, secretary, and treasurer of their union and won. This gave them a seat on the contract bargaining committee, a literal seat at the table in decision making. We encourage union participation among all teachers interested in policy and decision making that happens beyond their classroom. For at least half of teachers, those in unionized settings, there is an institutional process that exists for teacher voice: it is through the union. We need more teachers who understand how policy works to be at that table.

2. **They mobilized their peers.** Teachers created the Elevate IPS campaign to draw attention and create a hub of action both in the city and online. They held storytelling workshops (using the strategies

(continued)

described in chapter 10) for almost 150 teachers. They recruited teachers to come to the simulation event described earlier. And they broadcast all of their actions on social media (see, for example, https://www.facebook.com/ElevateIPS/).

3. **They fought cuts in the state legislature.** At the same time that the teachers were working at the district level to undo the wage freeze, the state legislature proposed $32 million in cuts to Indiana Public Schools. The teachers took their case to the legislature to explain how the money would be used, and helped to get more than half of the proposed cuts restored, enabling the district to commit to the salary improvements.

4. **They took to the media.** Four of the lead teachers in the Elevate IPS campaign, along with the district superintendent, wrote an op-ed piece that appeared in the major local paper, the *Indianapolis Star.* A half dozen additional teachers wrote articles telling their personal story and the story of how the pay freeze had negatively affected their schools and students.

5. **They had well-respected teachers as leaders of the campaign.** As we established in the previous chapter, policy leaders don't see all teachers as equally valuable to student learning. Some of the teachers who had stepped up to lead the effort had won the most prestigious awards in the district, lending status to the campaign.

Teachers can play a role in how districts make spending decisions. To do so, you need to be able to ask the right questions about the context, work to obtain information teachers don't generally have, and make a game plan for how to proceed. And remember, no one is touching the whole elephant. If the dollars will affect you and your students, find your way to the table.

A Beginner's Guide to Understanding Resource Allocation

The stories from Indianapolis and Chicago are on-the-ground examples. What should you know about the macro story on spending as it relates to teachers? What should you know if you are looking to be the catalyst for spending in a different way? For the sake of specificity, let's assume you're interested in finding funding for teacher leadership. If you don't have the ERS simulation to give you real costs, what might you do?

We've established that policymaking means perpetually operating in an environment of scarce resources. There will never be enough money to provide every student with every support that could be beneficial to his or her learning. How then does one start to form an opinion about how resources are being allocated?

How can a nonexpert evaluate whether specific state education budgets, specific school districts, and specific education program areas are adequately funded? There are a few basics that provide macro-level context for better understanding resources. I'll start by outlining those here and then transition to a game plan teachers can use to wade into advocacy that involves resources.

I'd like to start with two disclaimers. First, I am not a finance, economics, or budgeting expert. My goal is to offer you a starting point, Education Resources 101. Second, I urge you to know your limits in advocacy. Budgets represent the complex intersection of the multiple levels and multiple agencies that make up the American education system. It is easy to get out of your depth—for example, trying to fight a local budget line item that cannot be removed because it is mandated by state law, or advocating for the state to add a line item to the education budget when that program is already funded, but through a different agency.

That said, what do we know about resources?

1. **Overall in the United States, education spending has increased substantially in the past generation.** As the role of the federal government grew in education, starting with the Civil Rights Act and later the creation of a federal Department of Education, per-pupil spending rose across the nation. For more than thirty years, education spending experienced a steady upward trajectory. For perspective, between 1970 and 2010, annual federal spending grew from $2.9 billion to $73.3 billion (when the federal stimulus [ARRA] pushed spending to record levels). The greatest increases were in special education spending.[2]

2. **Most states are spending less today than they were before the 2008 recession.** Although education spending is up over the long term, states and districts are currently struggling under conditions

of relative deprivation. In the forty-six states for which there are data, the overwhelming majority—thirty-one states—were working with less funding per pupil in 2014 than they were in 2008. In at least fifteen states, the gap between spending levels in 2008 and 2014 amounted to a loss of more than 10 percent of the total budget.[3] These dramatic budget shortfalls often necessitate policy action—and often actions that are unwelcome in classrooms.

3. **Education spending in the United States is comparable to Western European nations with better student outcomes.** A common refrain among education reformers is that we are at or near the top of all industrialized nations for spending, but in the middle of the pack at best on measurements of student learning. The data bear out this narrative.

4. **Some school systems in the United States are adequately funded; others are not.** Any debate about adequacy of funding has to be a local one. As described in chapter 3, there are eye-popping differences between states in education spending (recall that New York's spending is more than three times higher than Idaho's) and even in neighboring districts (recall Chicago Ridge and Rondout in Illinois). The fact that property taxes are a key source of school funding drives between-district inequality of resources.

    Funding adequacy does not always break down neatly along income lines, with the schools serving more affluent students having greater per-pupil allocations. Consider that Newark, New Jersey, spends a whopping $30,671 per pupil, though its high school graduation rates are lower[4] than another major US urban center, Clark County (Las Vegas), Nevada, which has only $7,745 to spend per pupil.[5]

5. **Funding increases benefit low-income students[6] (but that does not stop debate on whether more funding is needed).** Over the past few years, several studies have presented compelling evidence that absolute dollars matter, especially for poor students. Consider the following summary of a study published by the National Bureau of Economic Research (NBER):

Between 1971 and 2010, supreme courts in 28 states responded to large gaps between richer and poorer school districts by *reforming school finance systems*. For low-income students who spent all 12 years of school in districts that increased spending by 20 percent, graduation rates rose by 23 percentage points. The estimates are based on the study's analysis of 15,000 children born between 1955 and 1985. The paper's analysis also found that low-income children who were exposed to a 20 percent spending increase for their entire school careers attained nearly a full year of additional education after high school. Between the ages of 25 and 45, these same children were 20 percentage points less likely to fall into poverty during any given year.[7]

Despite the short-term and long-term benefits shown to be associated with increased investment for low-income students, debate rages on whether *more money* or *better use* of money is needed. For every study like NBER's, there is a highly visible Newark example that prompts the public to question whether the increased investment will yield dividends for students.

Given this basic information about school finance, how might you move forward to evaluate and possibly advocate for a better use of resources on the issue that matters to you? Here is a set of suggestions that will guide you through the first steps.

Do Your Homework and Ask Good Questions

Your primary takeaway from the previous section is that policymakers will not be persuaded by the argument that every challenge in the education system must be addressed with more money. The question of whether more funding is actually needed is location specific and issue specific. Advocacy for funding something new is about making a case. That case should involve stories of your experience and that of your students, but these stories should be set in the larger context. To create the case for your issue, investigate the following:

- Is spending in your district higher or lower than in the surrounding communities?

- Is spending in your district higher or lower than in districts of similar size?

- What do other districts spend to run the program you want to run? At what scale? Do costs go up or down over time?

- What are the items in the existing district budget that you perceive to be wasteful? (Maybe there are expenses you would like to advocate cutting, but you probably will first need to gather more information about them if you are to make your case.)

- What, exactly, do the line items in your district budget mean? (Often, the categories are opaque and don't easily translate to the way you would organize school costs in your head. For example, there may be a category for "instructional expenses" that includes not just teacher salaries but also books and other teaching materials and supplies. Often, the salaries of regular education teachers are separate from those of special education teachers. Again, it is easy to get out of your depth of understanding and make the wrong assumptions on your own.)

- What are the state laws that relate to your issue, and how is spending on your issue constrained? Is there anything in your local contract that will facilitate or inhibit your issue?

Although you can obtain the answers to the first few questions with a simple Google search, matters of finance and budgeting are good areas in which to enlist the help of your local union where possible. Union leaders can help you obtain information and find colleagues who share your passion for a particular issue.

Go for What You Know

Some parts of a district or state budget are more ripe for teacher input than others. There are areas that affect teachers more directly, where teacher voice can be instrumental in helping a district make better use of available funds. Spending on teacher professional development (PD) is an area worth highlighting here. States and districts spend massive sums of money on PD for teachers, yet most teachers report that the PD they receive is not worth their time.

A study by the nonprofit TNTP estimates that we spend an average of $18,000 per teacher per year on PD, which amounts to $8 billion annually in the fifty largest US districts alone.[8] Wow, right?!

If you were in charge, how might you spend those dollars differently to make sure they resulted in real changes in the classroom? With Teach Plus, teachers in several cities have advocated for more teacher-led PD in their districts. Teachers who can demonstrate a specific area of expertise teach courses, typically five weeks long, to other teachers. They develop new lessons together, go back and try them out in the classroom, and participate in a cycle of inquiry around strategies to best engage students around a particular topic.

> Changing resource allocation, or policy generally, is about finding entry points.

Changing resource allocation, or policy generally, is about finding entry points. In the case of PD spending, most district leaders would acknowledge that those dollars could be put to better use. This creates an opportunity (or entry point) for teachers to be a part of developing a fix that is better for both teachers and students.

Think Outside the Box

The first stop on your path to figuring out how to fund the issue you care about might be your district budget, but it should not be your last. There are federal, state, and district grant programs, some of which are targeted toward teachers.

In addition to competitive government grant programs, there are many philanthropically funded grant programs available. Philanthropic donations to education exceed $1 billion annually.[9] Although that is only a fraction of the $600 billion spent on US education each year, it is more than enough to fund your pilot program. There is a spectrum of donors with a wide range of resources available and a wide range of funding priorities. On one end of this spectrum is the Bill and Melinda Gates Foundation, the largest private foundation in the world with an almost $45 billion endowment.[10] On the other end is my dad, a retired teacher, who asks each of his adult children to contribute a hundred bucks each year to offer a small scholarship in memory of my deceased mom. In between are literally thousands of individuals and organizations that make charitable contributions to education.

Like the federal government, major philanthropists seek to have an outsize influence with their limited dollars by asking districts to align the existing budgets to achieve the goals of the grant. In a recent example that's familiar to many, funding to support Common Core implementation has been a heavy philanthropic investment, available only to districts that were prioritizing adoption of the standards.

The T3 Initiative referenced in chapter 5, originally developed and proposed by a group of teachers in Boston, helped the district garner both competitive grants from the state and philanthropic dollars. A viable idea that came from teachers helped the district bring in new revenue to support teachers and students.

A final way to think outside the box involves examining education spending relative to spending on other social services. While education spending has grown over time, spending on our prison systems has grown almost three times faster.[11] Most of us would agree that growing our prison system faster than our education system does not reflect the priorities we would want for our nation. Thus the question becomes, How can we make commitments in education that could steer dollars back to preventing incarceration—by improving schools?

⁊　⁊　⁊

In the policy world of imperfect information, resource decisions are made with both hearts and minds. Think back to the example of the Indianapolis teachers earlier in the chapter. They helped forge a new contract with pay raises because they were able to combine their stories with clear opinions (from a large group of teachers) about the trade-offs the district should make to achieve a balanced budget. All teachers have dozens of indelible stories to bring forth that can win over hearts. The challenge is to pair those stories with information that wins over the minds of policymakers.

Key Takeaways

☐ Resource allocation is central to policymaking, but an area in which most teachers have little experience meaningfully participating.

☐ In terms of resources, the policy question is not "Is it good for kids?" because many, many programs could support students. The question is "Is this the highest-leverage way to spend limited school dollars?"

☐ There is significant disparity between districts and between states in terms of funding. Some locations are funded more adequately than others, though most districts in America have experienced funding cuts since the recession of 2008.

☐ Increased funding in low-income districts has been demonstrated to raise student outcomes, though there are districts where funding adequacy has not translated into student success.

☐ Teachers can successfully advocate for changes in resource allocation, but doing so will involve learning enough about district spending to offer concrete suggestions about the trade-offs involved in balancing a budget.

Notes

1. The world doesn't operate as neatly as the simulation I've described. I can see only my side of the elephant—in this case, how much teachers can rise to the occasion and make meaningful contributions to budget policy when they have the information and tools to do so. It is also true that a budget process is never just about budgeting. Politics overlay the process. Teachers can certainly recognize that cuts need to be made. At the same time, they can disagree with the metrics used to determine which schools to close. It could also be true that the mayor was determined to shrink traditional district schools in favor of growing charter schools. We'll get to politics and power in chapter 9; understanding resource allocation comes first.
2. Dan Lips and Shanea Watkins, *Does Spending More on Education Improve Academic Achievement?* (Washington, DC: Heritage Foundation, September 2008).
3. Lauren Camera, "State Education Funding Hasn't Recovered from Recession," *US News and World Report*, December 10, 2015, http://www.usnews.com/news/blogs/data-mine/2015/12/10/ state-education-funding-hasnt-recovered-from-recession.
4. Carla Astudillo, "What's Your School District's Graduation Rate? Explore the New Data," nj.com (December 20, 2013), http://www.nj.com/news/index .ssf/2013/12/interactive_graduation_rates_for_inner-city_schools_low_ vocational_schools_come_out_on_top.html.
5. Neal Morton, "CCSD Grad Rate Inches Up," *Las Vegas Review Journal*, October 15, 2015, http://www.reviewjournal.com/education/ ccsd-grad-rate-inches.
6. C. Kirabo Jackson, Rucker Johnson, and Claudia Persico, *The Effect of School Finance Reforms on the Distribution of Spending, Academic Achievement and Adult Outcomes*, NBER Working Paper No. 20118 (Washington, DC: National Bureau of Economic Research, 2014), http://www.nber.org/papers/w20118.
7. Holly Yettick, "School Spending Increases Linked to Better Outcomes for Poor Students," *Education Week*, May 29, 2014.
8. New Teacher Project, *The Mirage: Confronting the Hard Truth about Our Quest for Teacher Development*, TNTP, http://tntp.org/assets/documents/ TNTP-Mirage_2015.pdf.

9. Sarah Reckhow, *Follow the Money: How Foundation Dollars Change Public School Politics* (Oxford: Oxford University Press, 2012).

10. Bill and Melinda Gates Foundation, "Who We Are: Annual Reports," http://www.gatesfoundation.org/Who-We-Are/Resources-and-Media/ Annual-Reports.

11. Stephanie Stullich, Ivy Morgan, and Oliver Schak, *State and Local Expenditures on Corrections and Education: A Brief from the U.S. Department of Education* (July 2016), http://www2.ed.gov/rschstat/eval/ other/expenditures-corrections-education/brief.pdf.

CHAPTER · SEVEN
Accountability

LESSON
Accountability Is Inescapable

I magine having to teach without standards or a basic curriculum. You'd likely think: *What the heck am I even supposed to accomplish here? How do I focus myself? How do I figure out if I'm operating at the right level of expectation?* Standards and curriculum are basic building blocks of teaching. Without them, your work would have far less impact.

Accountability is an essential building block in the work of policymakers. It is the third leg of the playing field triangle I introduced in chapter 4. Accountability is the mechanism that focuses policymakers on the question of what needs to get accomplished. Accountability asks, What are taxpayers getting for their dollar?

Accountability has become a dirty word in education. I'd lay odds that in any chance meeting of a teacher and a policymaker, testing would make its way into the conversation, and the parties would have differing points of view.

The teacher would most likely be concerned about individual students and the time that testing takes and ask, "Why do we need state testing anyhow? It just limits instructional time for my kids."

The policymaker would most likely respond, "How do we know if we're closing achievement gaps if we're not checking student progress? How can I make the case in the legislature for more funding for education if I can't quantify the problem and show evidence of interventions that make a difference?"

This conversation symbolizes the polarized world in which we're currently stuck. I believe that teachers need to get involved in fixing accountability, but as I mentioned in chapter 2, they can't just be the party of no.

In this chapter, I'll lay out my basic beliefs on the issue of accountability and how teachers can play a role in improving how it happens. In summary, they are as follows:

- Accountability is going to exist, and testing will be a part of it.
- Testing is broken, in part because we didn't involve teachers in its design.
- We need informed teacher advocates at the table to help fix testing.
- The greatest threat to getting teachers at the policy table for the long term is sometimes other teachers.

I'll conclude with examples from my home state of Massachusetts that illustrate how two different groups of teachers approached advocacy around the future of accountability. I'll offer my analysis of what these disparate efforts accomplished and their implications for future teacher advocacy.

Accountability Is Going to Exist, and Testing Will Be a Part of It

As I noted in Chapter 4, half of state tax dollars in most states are spent on education. Policymakers are ultimately responsible for being able to show taxpayers that this money is being invested wisely and that students are learning more and better than they have in the past. Thus policymakers are motivated to fund programs and school models that are tied to tangible results, especially in terms of student test scores. This approach has had both positive and negative consequences in schools.

In a resource-scarce system whose goal is to serve all students, questions about whether funded programs are having the desired effect will never go away. Hoping that a policymaker will give up on pursuing accountability and evidence for the good use of tax dollars is like hoping that a teacher will give up on individual students. It is baked into their DNA. Pressure to hold schools accountable—stated differently, to be able to tell taxpayers that their dollars are being spent wisely—is fundamental to the role.

Accountability in education, of course, means much more than how students do on standardized tests. But student learning is the singular top-line goal of schools. Thus the questions of how to measure student learning, how often to measure it and on what topics, and what the bar for proficiency should be, among others, are central in policymaking.

The Every Student Succeeds Act encourages states to broaden the categories used to hold schools accountable, so as to avoid a disproportionate emphasis on tests. I recently observed two teachers make a brilliant case for why student attendance is a critical metric that has often been overlooked in state accountability systems. I agree. Many make the case for monitoring noncognitive measures of development as rigorously as those for math and ELA. Incorporating additional measures for judging school progress is an important step in the evolution of accountability.

Still, plenty of educators argue that measuring schools based on tests is altogether the wrong metric. The NEA, for example, is trying to turn the tables on an accountability system driven by student outcomes by focusing on holding school systems accountable for providing students with access to

- Optimal ratios of specialized instructional support personnel (school counselors, social workers, nurses, psychologists)
- Class sizes that allow for one-on-one attention
- Health, social-emotional, and wellness programs
- High-quality early education programs
- Full-day, five-day-a-week kindergarten

The question then becomes, how would you make the case for the funding increases to support the investments on their list?

If you think that schools should receive more funding to support the greater struggles of poor students, fighting against testing is actually likely to hurt your case for increased funding. Take a look at this summary of a well-respected piece of research released in February 2016.

> A new working paper by the National Bureau of Economic Research, joins a fairly large body of research showing that spending more in schools improves student outcomes—that is, money matters. The study uses national testing data to see what happens after a state alters its school finance system [such that] resources are directed to low-income districts. Specifically they examine reforms in 27 states since 1990, and conclude that student achievement increased as a result.[1]

This is good news for those of us who believe that poor students need greater resources than they are currently receiving if they are to have an equitable shot at success in school. The report even makes it clear that spending on "non-instructional purposes" like "student support services" has value. What is noteworthy, however, is not that evidence exists to support this notion. What is noteworthy is *what* evidence is presented. The conclusions are drawn based on student test score data. Investing more money in, and offering more programs related to, student support services yields greater student academic achievement. This type of research makes the compelling case that is needed to drive better resource allocation to schools serving students with the greatest needs. You can't make this case to policymakers without test data.

Want more money to help high-poverty schools battle the challenges of poverty? Show that the investment makes a difference in terms of student learning. Tests speak the language of policy.

The flip side of that lesson is, Want to make sure that poor schools are starved of the additional funds they need to serve students? Fight the testing and accountability systems that would show where greater resources are needed.

Testing Is Broken, in Part Because We Didn't Involve Teachers in Its Design

Recall the concept of unintended consequences discussed in chapter 4. The federal role in establishing annual testing in most grades—and the concurrent expectation that all students reach grade-level proficiency by 2014—originated with the passage of the No Child Left Behind Act (NCLB). NCLB is a study in unintended consequences. In its case, policy was a blanket of uniform expectations spread over the uneven surface of American schools.

NCLB offered a defined end goal for testing—every student proficient—but did not specify the route that states had to take to get there. Policy that is "tight on ends and loose on means" is typical and arguably smart. Annual testing seemed like a commonsense mandate. Most states were already giving tests at many grade levels. States that did annual testing were beginning to produce data that shed clearer light than ever before on the achievement gap, allowing for better targeting of resources. In the words of former US representative George Miller (D-CA), "We simply wanted the states to tell us how their students were performing on whatever test the states were giving at the specified grade points and to disaggregate the data so that we would know how all students were progressing."

Although a rule that is tight on ends but loose on means does achieve flexibility, it fails to provide important guidance to those charged with implementation and then held accountable. The originators of NCLB may have envisioned states simply giving one annual test per grade and then learning from the data; however, their lack of guidance on such issues as the frequency of tests, the qualities of worthwhile tests, and who should decide on which tests to administer led to a cascade of unintended consequences. Being loose on the means to achieving an accountability end created the space for unintended consequences to sneak in.

The following are some of the unintended consequences of NCLB's brand of "loose-tight," which we are still trying to rectify today:

- States could set their own definitions of "proficiency"; some set the bar much lower than others.
- States and districts needed ongoing information on student progress to ensure that they were moving toward proficiency, so they added benchmark and formative assessments.
- The law's mandated timelines and expected degree of improvement resulted in rushed test adoption processes that rarely involved teacher input.

NCLB's testing requirement may have started out with a simple logic, but it mutated, becoming increasingly irrational over time. By 2015—the spring before the Every Student Succeeds Act (ESSA) passed to replace NCLB and at the height of the testing opt-out movement—most teachers were living a doctoral-level course in the unintended consequences of policy.

1. The tests often didn't align to the standards that teachers were expected to teach. This problem was exacerbated by the introduction of the new Common Core State Standards (CCSS), as the tests in use were still the ones built around the old standards.

2. Test results didn't come back until the next school year, making it impossible to use them in diagnosis and remediation of student learning challenges.

3. Often, the interim and benchmark tests that districts used did not test the same things as the end-of-year exams.

4. Too often, districts and schools used instructional time to run classes in test-taking skills or hold pep rallies centered around achieving great test scores.

Two straws related to testing landed on the proverbial camel's back at the same time. The first was the new assessments aligned to the CCSS, widely perceived as *another* test that would get added, rather than as a replacement for outdated state tests. The second was the rise in the use of student test data in teacher evaluations. For teachers, these two issues felt like, *So you're going to squeeze out all of the time I have to teach my students with testing, then give them a brand-new assessment that I've never seen and fire me if they don't perform well? Great.*

We Need Teachers at the Table to Help Fix Testing

I believe there is no single issue in education with a greater need for teacher voice than testing. In my role, I see the huge gulf between policy intent and teacher reality. I also have the opportunity to peer into lots of districts and charter schools and see glimmers of hope. Despite the problems, I deeply believe that the problem of fixing testing in America is solvable, and that it can only be solved with teachers leading the way. Teachers involved with Teach Plus have come up with some pretty cool ideas that point a path forward.

As we enter the era of the ESSA, the good news is that policy leaders have confirmed, in the law, their intent to limit the amount of time students spend taking tests. The legislation allocates funding so that states can audit the assessments they give and get feedback from practitioners on issues like the tests' usefulness in improving instruction, the timing and the format of the data teachers receive from the tests, and whether there is adequate technology to administer the test. Funds can even be used to help districts get out of contracts for assessments judged to be of low value. As of early 2016, thirty-two states had made public commitments to review the tests students were taking, with the intention of reducing the amount. With ESSA, there is now a direct, funded opportunity to improve how accountability is implemented, and state policymakers are taking the opportunity seriously.

Further, ESSA specifies that teachers need to be at the table for key accountability decisions. Policymakers don't know how to fix the problems that exist on the ground in schools. That can be done only with teacher voice and perspective.

A Tale of Two Teacher Advocacy Efforts

I'm now going to tell two stories of teacher voice from Massachusetts. They involve two different groups of teachers simultaneously advocating for differing sides of the same issue.

In 2015, the Massachusetts Board of Elementary and Secondary Education planned to vote on whether to adopt the PARCC (Partnership for Assessment of Readiness for College and Careers) tests statewide. Since the 1990s, Massachusetts had been lauded for its standards and locally focused assessment system, the MCAS (Massachusetts Comprehensive Assessment System). However, as the state adopted the new CCSS in 2010, there was no longer alignment between what teachers were expected to teach and the tests they gave. Enter the PARCC assessments aligned to the CCSS. For teachers, there was an open question: Are the PARCC assessments right for my students, especially considering the turbulence that would come with switching to them?

Enlisting Teacher Expertise to Fix Testing

At Teach Plus, we worked with a group of excellent teachers to figure out how to engage lots of teachers across the state in the issue. In the early planning, the group identified the answers to two key strategy questions:

- What is the unique expertise of teachers?
- What new information do teachers need to be effective advocates?

Teachers determined that they were uniquely positioned to be able to weigh in on which tests were better aligned to what they were expected to teach. The group also recognized a need for more information. Most teachers had limited exposure to PARCC test items and could not advocate one way or another without more exposure to the content of the test.

We worked to create daylong events for teachers that combined professional development and opportunities to have input on the future of testing. At tables with other teachers, the participants examined PARCC test items for their grade and subject, and judged them against the CCSS for their grade and subject. At the end of the day, teachers participated in live polling about their opinions of the tests. Almost twelve hundred teachers participated.

On average, a strong majority (79 percent) of teachers said the new tests were higher quality and measured the things they cared about for their students, such as critical thinking skills and alignment to standards. The teacher leaders who developed the events used this polling information in testimony before the State Board of Elementary and Secondary Education, in op-eds in local newspapers, and in meetings with education leaders.

In the final days before the Massachusetts vote, the commissioner of education proposed a compromise: create a new test that retains the local character of the MCAS but borrows heavily from the PARCC to ensure alignment to the current standards. Massachusetts remained in the consortium of "PARCC states," but would create a test just for itself.

What did this approach to teacher advocacy accomplish?

In the complex world of policy, there are a number of ways to analyze the success and failure of a particular initiative. Let's consider a few of the accomplishments:

Teacher-led information campaign   Teachers involved in the effort recognized that the most important thing their organizing could offer was the opportunity for other teachers to become prepared to use the new test. The opportunity for access to test items drove teacher participation. This effort appealed to teachers' sense of professionalism.

Authentic input on a key policy question   Teachers were invited into dozens of conversations with board members, the media, and other leaders because they had knowledge that others could not offer, and were seeking to help answer the single question that was on the table for the board: *Which* test should be adopted?

An example of solution-oriented action by a group of mostly union teachers   In a world where decision makers often worry that inviting teachers to the table means inviting the party of no, these teachers took a constructive approach.

Continued participation by the state in the PARCC consortium The state could continue to draw test items from PARCC's item banks and to structure the test and its categories in similar ways.

What Did This Approach to Teacher Advocacy Fail to Accomplish?

A settled testing debate in the state After one year of using the PARCC, students would need to transfer again to yet another new test. The teachers' effort could not overcome the politics surrounding the issue, and thus they could not shield their students from yet another year of change.

A unified voice among teachers Although more than a thousand teachers participated in this effort in a variety of ways, they did not represent the dominant voice on the issue. The board was making its decision with a powerful national opt-out movement as its backdrop. While these teachers were weighing in on the question of which test to give, a separate contingent of teachers was trying to change the question altogether to one of whether state testing should be eliminated.

This brings me to my final point of the chapter and the story about the second group of teachers. *The greatest threat to getting teachers to the policy table for the long term is sometimes other teachers.*

Mobilizing Teachers to Stop Testing

During the year leading up to the PARCC vote, teachers aligned to the opt-out movement captured regular news attention for their vociferous opposition to standardized testing. Some of the leaders advancing the antitesting agenda were also top leaders in their unions. Their messaging obscured (purposely, in my estimation) the real question being decided by the state board and shifted attention to opting out. To other teachers and the public, they framed the fact that the state was making a decision on testing (a possible snooze) as a call to action for a moratorium on high-stakes testing (a nonsnooze to teachers giving too many tests).

Their rhetoric connected the issue at hand—whether the PARCC would be adopted—to a completely separate issue that was of interest to many teachers but a nonstarter among policymakers: a testing moratorium for the state. The connection was visible in the slogans seen in online memes and on signs at public hearings, such as "No PARCCing" (with the universal "no" symbol of a red circle with a line through it) and "Less Testing, More Learning."

National momentum around opt-out fostered a galvanizing moment among many teachers in Massachusetts. Teachers turned out in droves to speak in support of a moratorium on high-stakes testing, despite the fact that such a moratorium was never even remotely under consideration by those on the state board making the decision. Framed as an opportunity to end the accountability they faced in their jobs, this issue was an easy rallying point for many teachers.

The effort, to some degree, was a success. What was once assumed to be a smooth ride for PARCC adoption in Massachusetts became a rocky battle that made national headlines.

What did this approach to teacher advocacy accomplish?
On a few different fronts, opt-out advocates could declare victory and advance that victory as a means of building greater momentum to further defeat testing in the future. The following were two important accomplishments:

Teacher solidarity and energy   In an era of declining union membership and declining active union participation, the amount of teacher participation and the degree of energy on the issue were noteworthy. Fighting testing is a "least common denominator" issue that is an ideal one around which to organize teachers. Framing the question as "Would you rather have accountability or no accountability?" gets people on your side. This case shows that you can build support even if a question is not, in fact, on the table.

A (misleading) talking point to build advocacy momentum   Every war is won in a series of individual battles. Ensuring that PARCC did not get fully adopted in Massachusetts could be presented as concrete evidence of success against the big corporations like Pearson that earn revenue when kids take state tests. PARCC cost substantial money to develop, and teacher voice played an important role in impeding its rollout in Massachusetts. That might get counted as a victory against the corporate testing regime and suggest that momentum was building toward the larger issue of ending high-stakes testing. However, as the next section demonstrates, this is far from a fair portrayal of events.

What did this approach to teacher advocacy fail to accomplish?
Although defeating full PARCC adoption was a victory on the surface to be
sure, anyone looking a little deeper would think twice. It is a classic Pyrrhic
victory, likely to do more harm than good to three of the causes that antitesting advocates hold dear: (1) thwarting the corporate testing regime for
making profits on public education, (2) ensuring that dollars are spent on
a well-rounded set of supports to develop the whole child in schools, and
(3) ensuring that teachers are empowered to have a real voice in decision
making. Let's take each of these topics in turn.

Cutting off the money supply to testing companies   Even though
adoption of the previously created and paid-for PARCC tests was
rejected, there was no movement on the larger issue that galvanized
teachers. State testing for Massachusetts would, of course, remain. Not
adopting PARCC as is simply meant that instead of reaping the benefit
of sharing costs with a large group of states, as was the case with the
PARCC, the state would need to create new contracts with testing companies to develop entirely new assessments. This time the state would
be wholly responsible for shouldering the cost of developing a new test
just for its own students. The expense of new test development could
reach in to the tens of millions. A far cry from stopping the gravy train
of public school dollars to testing companies, this decision created a
new need for spending on tests, just as the expensive development of
PARCC ended.

**Ensuring that greater school spending goes to meet an array of stu-
dent needs**   Advocates motivated teacher action by pitting spending
on a test against spending on students. The implied connection in their
campaign was that stopping PARCC would add time and money for
educators to better serve students. In fact, in addition to the new dollars
lost to classrooms for the development of an entirely new test, students
also lose time and focus in the educator community. Instead of focusing
on getting better at using a test already being administered, teachers
across the state will be spending time developing, (inevitably fighting),
and then learning the expectations of a new test.

Securing teachers a voice in decision making   In the Massachusetts
debates, teacher voice was in the foreground, but the antitesting voice
was not on point in the discussion at hand and was often obstructionist.

Their position on PARCC came after years of being at the table under prior leadership and supporting the implementation of the CCSS and its new aligned tests.

,   ,   ,

The stories I've related offer compelling evidence that teacher voice matters—especially on pivotal issues like accountability.

From my vantage point, teachers need to choose their battles when it comes to tests. You can't be fighting to improve the quality of tests at the same time that you are fighting to eliminate them. Those are separate goals. Although the new federal law and all states require annual tests, some teachers are encouraging disregard for law. For example, the home page on the Massachusetts Teachers' Association website has a large banner that reads, "Supporting opt-out is one of the strongest statements we can make as educators against standardized testing." This, despite the fact that the federal government requires 95 percent of students in a state to participate in state testing, or the state risks the loss of hundreds of millions of dollars in federal funds.

The maxim "If you're not at the table, you're on the menu" is certainly true of teachers when it comes to policy.

When a large organizing body encourages its members to take an action that puts state education officials at risk of not being able to deliver much-needed dollars to their state, the effect is one of declaring war. Those same officials have significant latitude in deciding whether and which teachers to bring to the table almost all of the time. (Recall my example in chapter 1 of how often the commissioner consulted me, his staffer, for "teacher voice.") The maxim "If you're not at the table, you're on the menu" is certainly true of teachers when it comes to policy.

For some, it appears that the goals are to end testing and accountability and go back to the days before we monitored whether schools were playing a positive role in helping kids learn. That toothpaste is never going back in the tube. Data play too big a role in education decision making, and in all other policy decision making for that matter. In many ways, the greatest threat to teachers having a stronger voice at the policymaking table is teachers. Fighting basic accountability will likely result in fewer opportunities for teachers to be consulted in policy decision making.

Key Takeaways

☐ Accountability is going to exist, and testing will be a part of it.

☐ Testing is broken, in part because we didn't involve teachers in its design.

☐ We need informed teacher advocates at the table to help fix testing.

☐ The greatest threat to getting teachers at the policy table for the long term is sometimes other teachers.

☐ The maxim "If you're not at the table, you're on the menu" is one teachers should consider as they plot their advocacy strategy.

Note

1. Matt Barnum, "New Research: States That Chose (or Were Forced) to Spend More Money on Poor Schools Saw Student Gains," *The 74* (February 22, 2016), https://www.the74million.org/article/new-research-states-that-chose-or-were-forced-to-spend-more-money-on-poor-schools-saw-student-gains.

Individuals and Groups

*There Is No Such Thing as One
Best Policy for All*

This chapter begins with a non-sellout teacher advocacy story.

On Sunday, May 21, 2011, my organization made the front page of the Sunday *New York Times*. I knew it was coming. Teach Plus had been in the *Times* the year before in an article that celebrated our Boston teachers for designing a program to recruit and train teams of teacher leaders to support improvement in low-performing schools. As the teacher-designed program was implemented, the national media took note.

Our teacher leadership work in cities like Indianapolis and Boston was starting to catch the attention of major national newspapers and the online community. Using our teachers as the example, they were starting to recognize and tell a powerful new story about teachers as problem solvers. There had been a number of stories to that point, and they had almost all been positive, sending a compelling message about the power of teachers— my dream for the organization come true. Part of that narrative was about a new generation of teachers who had become the majority in US classrooms. In 2011, we released research demonstrating that, after almost forty years of Baby Boomers as the majority of the teaching force, the demographic tide had turned, and teachers with less than ten years' experience had become the majority. This new majority of relative novices was shaking things up in exciting ways.

When we had launched our policy fellowship in Indianapolis two years earlier, I asked the group of teachers my standard opening question: "What changes do you think are needed to better serve students and keep great teachers like you?" As we went around the room, almost every teacher said, "Stop laying us off every year." They went on to describe in detail what it was like to want to teach in the system but to perpetually lack any kind of job security or stability. Teachers told stories of building strong relationships at one school only to be "RIF'd" (the acronym for reduction in force, or layoff) in spring, spend the summer unemployed, and land in a new school just at the start of the term. Others had moved to charter schools or the more stable districts that surrounded Indianapolis Public Schools (IPS).

One of the most compelling stories came from Abby Taylor. She was a fifth-year teacher who had been RIF'd every year. Both she and her husband, who was also a teacher, were RIF'd in 2011. Right after she got pregnant. Right after they bought their first home. Both of them had grown up in low-income communities themselves and were committed to the students of IPS, but they had no safety net or prospects of stability to show for their five years of commitment to the district.

These stories drove their work as policy fellows over the next two years.

Fortunately, Abby and some of the other teachers who became active in creating a more stable work environment for early-career teachers were active in their unions. In fact, Abby was the secretary of her union. Our local Teach Plus executive director, Casey Patterson, had come to us from a union leadership position.

In 2010, the group worked within the union to initiate a joint committee with the district on modifications to the layoff process. Later that spring, the committee agreed on a new system for determining layoffs, which took both seniority and teacher performance into account. In the new system, seniority still played a greater role than performance. The union executive board voted on the change and endorsed it.

A year later, in 2011, sweeping changes moved through the Indiana state legislature. The changes were similar to those being signed into law across the nation, spurred in part by the $4.5 billion Race to the Top grants that promised big money to states that could lead the way toward a modern teaching profession that rewarded teachers based on their performance.

In Indiana, an omnibus bill, SEA 1, passed, introducing new expectations around teacher evaluation, career ladders, pay, and layoff processes. Unlike the city contract of a year earlier, this bill made performance, rather than seniority, the tiebreaking factor in layoff decisions.

Teach Plus fellows had roles on state cabinets defining the proposed changes, and did things like write op-eds and give testimony before the legislature. Their position was that changes were necessary to prevent a hollowing out of the teaching force in the city. Those with midrange experience (two to seven years) were getting laid off every year, leaving only an aging crop of very veteran teachers and the annual rotation of first-years. Although the debate over whether performance or seniority should be the tiebreaking factor in layoffs got lots of media attention, the issue was not of primary concern to most of the teachers. To them, performance just needed to play some role.

Sam Dillon, the Pulitzer Prize–winning *New York Times* reporter assigned to the story, flew to Indianapolis to learn more about SEA 1.

He learned about the training we do, helping teachers understand how policy works, analyze policy research and best practices from other cities and states, and home in on the issues they care about. He visited class-rooms in Indy and learned about the testimony our teachers had given, stepping out of their comfort zones to fight for their jobs, their students, and the future of the teaching force in IPS.

In a nutshell, the teachers' advocacy was a challenge to a notion implic-itly held by most Americans, the notion that there is One Best System.

The Myth of the One Best System

You are probably reading this book because you believe that change in edu-cation is necessary and possible. You have a vision of a system that serves students better than our current model does. Right?

David Tyack's book *The One Best System* has a well-earned place in the canon of required readings for students of the history and politics of edu-cation. In it, he documents the evolution of US schooling from the time of the village-controlled schoolhouse to the start of the modern reform era a generation ago. An implicit guiding belief that shapes the aspirations of many participants in school reform is captured clearly by the book's title. With the right policies, we can build One Best System.

It is not possible, of course. Our system grew up from locally controlled and widely varied beginnings.[1] We are a diverse country. Policy cannot stamp out that variation. But in the subconscious of most Americans is the aspirational notion that we can build the One Best System—except that, just like the definition of equity in the aspirational notion of "achieving equity in schools," the definition of "best" is subject to every individual's interpretation.

In reality, there are winners and losers in every policy decision that affects schools.

In reality, there are winners and losers in every policy decision that affects schools. The best system (that is, the best use of public resources) for suburban kids is not the best system for urban kids. The best system for a special education student is not the best system for a regular educa-tion student.

The Myth of Monolithic Teacher Voice

An extension of the notion of the One Best System is that there is one best version of the system for teachers. Most of the public, and teachers themselves, assume that teachers all share the same opinion on the basic elements of the One Best

Policy is a contest of ideas. Healthy professional associations need to find a way to embrace that and use it to their advantage.

System, despite evidence to the contrary. For example, the fact that each teacher's contract in the country varies from the next is little discussed, especially by teachers. The public generally sees teachers as speaking with one voice and having a shared best interest.

For decades, the majority of teachers have been members of unions. Speaking with one voice has served the profession well in earning fair pay and working conditions and in standing up to administration. As noted in chapter 2, for the forty-year stretch from the late 1960s to the early 2000s, Baby Boomers made up the majority in the teaching force. For them, teaching was a career they began in their twenties and, by and large, stayed with until retirement. A seniority-driven system that had teachers "waiting their turn" for plum class assignments, leadership roles in the union, and excellent retirement benefits fit the average teacher's career trajectory. A fifth-year teacher might be a "loser" under a seniority-driven system, paying her dues with challenging classrooms, lower pay, and little say in the union, but she knew she would be a "winner" in the future under the same policy.

What about the teacher who chooses to leave at the end of year 5 and never reaps the benefits of waiting her turn? The field in general had the luxury of not worrying about that person because she was the exception rather than the rule. From the teacher perspective in this bygone era, there arguably *was* one best system for a stable, thriving teaching profession. It worked. Teachers were part of a healthy middle class in the longest stretch of economic prosperity the nation has ever seen.

Today, many things have changed:

1. Short-term careers are the rule rather than the exception.
2. Research has made clear that more experience in teaching doesn't always correlate to being a better teacher.
3. Fewer than half of all teachers are union members.[2]

In a seniority-driven system like teaching, union leaders are disproportionately nearing retirement. As illustrated by the Indianapolis case, senior teachers' interests are sometimes at odds with those of newer teachers.

I believe that the collective voice that unions provide is critical to the strength of the teaching profession. Yet the union of today must wrestle with essential questions illustrated by the Indianapolis case. What should the collective voice be saying when the majority it speaks for has less than ten years' experience, and unions are rapidly losing market share, especially among younger teachers?

It is easier to lead all teachers with a message that there is one best policy for all. Unfortunately, the world of today is more complicated than that.

Policy is a contest of ideas. Healthy professional associations need to find a way to embrace this truth and use it to their advantage.

The Postscript on the *New York Times* Story

The story that appeared in the *Times* bore no resemblance to the story I thought would get published. It did not mention teachers by name. It did not reference visits to their classrooms.

Instead the article diminished the teachers' role in change and began from the premise that all teachers share a common vision of the One Best System. It told the reader to be suspicious of anything less than monolithic teacher voice. The author dismissed the notion that different subgroups of teachers could have different perspectives and work to modernize policies that affected their lives.

The article ended up being about the Bill and Melinda Gates Foundation and the role the foundation's philanthropy plays in education. The piece wasn't about working-class teachers trying to pay a mortgage and feed their babies because the best system for them looked different from the school systems of the past. That they were successful was evidence that it couldn't have been through their own efforts. Instead the article posited that they couldn't have done it without the Gates Foundation's clout.

The article questioned whether it is a good thing for philanthropists to support new ideas that challenge "the way things have always been done." I still go to Indy regularly and meet with the teachers who learned new skills, connected to new colleagues, stood up for themselves, and saved their jobs. I believe we need ways (which will include philanthropic support) to get new ideas into the conversation. I believe that in order to have healthy schools that change with the times, teachers need to participate in questioning the One Best System.

New Voices in a New Era

The reason Teach Plus had the lede in the *Times* was that having an organized group of teachers speak separately from a union, with a perspective that strayed from the typical union perspective, was unusual. What was lost in the story was that the Teach Plus fellows leading the effort *were also* leaders in their unions. From the story's perspective, they were organizing separately under the banner of Bill Gates. In fact, they were raising their hands within their union to lead difficult conversations within, while also participating in real-time policy conversations that were being debated in the statehouse. Many of those same teachers, including Abby Taylor, continue to teach and hold elected leadership roles in their unions today. They are passionate about helping the union survive and thrive, but they believe that that will require difficult changes.

These teachers offer four lessons for other teachers who are seeking change:

1. **Start the conversation in your union (where possible).** Not all teachers are members of unions, but those who are have the potential to lead

needed conversations within their own ranks. In the Indianapolis case, the union leadership was receptive to hearing what newer teachers had to say, and they were able to broker a compromise. Unions are democratic institutions; their leaders listen best when many teachers express interest in the same change.

2. **Seek out like-minded colleagues.** One thing that made these teachers different from the average teacher who wishes for change is that they had identified a group of allies with a common experience. **They had each other.** They had learned about how common their individual RIF stories were when they joined the fellowship and got to know the other teachers. Lots of teachers think that many of the decisions made and policies created outside their classrooms are crazy and misguided. Few have dedicated time to discuss which policies are hurting students and to figure out how to take action. These teachers could see that there were many losers in the teaching force under the current RIF policy.

3. **Do your homework.** A second characteristic of these teachers was that they had **knowledge** that most teachers don't have about the context beyond their classroom. They worked for two years to collect data on the problem. They had survey data which showed that over 70 percent of teachers in the district thought performance should factor into layoff decisions. They studied the research (covered in chapter 6) that was animating policymakers around the question of how to address equity for students by addressing teacher quality. They did their homework.

4. **Analyze how students will be affected.** What was in the teachers' interest—a fair path to ensure the future of the teaching force in the city—was also in the interest of students. The best interest of students was a focal motivation for them. When they were forced to move from school to school each year, they wound up as just another impermanent, unreliable figure in the lives of students who already had more than their share of those. When they watched a novice, beloved by students, leave teaching after being RIF'd, they mourned the loss of a potential colleague who could have lit up thousands of students over several decades. Of course, this interest also aligned better with the interest of policymakers who had equity, resources, and accountability on their minds.

The Decision Maker View of the One Best System

Whereas teachers have traditionally thought in terms of their collective interest, policymakers recognize that trade-offs are the very definition of their work:

Policy = Trade-offs

Whereas teachers may find it difficult to discuss the idea that with any given policy there are winners and losers among their ranks, this is the very substance of any policy discussion. To come to the table arguing that there is One Best System for all teachers is to come unprepared to answer the questions of those on the other side of that table. The policy-maker's job is to consider how resources might be reallocated in service of students. Thinking like a policymaker means thinking in terms of who wins and who loses.

> **Whereas teachers have traditionally thought in terms of their collective interest, policymakers recognize that trade-offs are the very definition of their work.**

Analyzing Trade-Offs, Winners, and Losers

There is a line of questioning that decision makers go through to surface trade-offs. Teachers would be well served to consider some of the same questions. A first stop for conversations like this, ideally, would be inside unions around the country.

- Is this particular policy good for students in my district?
- Which students will benefit the most?
- Which students might lose out?
- What do they stand to lose?
- What constituencies speak for and with student subgroups (for example, special education students)? What is their strength relative to other constituencies with other opinions?
- Can we afford it? What areas will lose funding to pay for this?

- Is it good for teachers on the whole?
- Which teachers will benefit the most?
- Will the teachers who benefit the least become a formidable opposition?

In Indianapolis, the teachers who benefited the least from seniority-based layoffs became a formidable opposition and led the way to changes in their union. This is still rare, but it is proof that this type of conversation among teachers with differing perspectives is possible.

I close the chapter with another example of how the One Best policy for teachers designed a generation ago may not be the One Best way now.

A Case Study in How One Best System for All Teachers Became a Losing Proposition for Most Teachers

My dad taught for thirty years in the same high school, owned his own home from the early days of his career, and raised six children on his income alone. He's been comfortably retired since his mid-fifties, enjoying the return on the three decades he invested in the classroom. His pension allows him to stay in his middle-class home, golf to excess, and, quite possibly, spend more years of his life collecting a pension check than a paycheck. His life embodies the essence of the American Dream circa 1969—the date when he entered the workforce. He had the good fortune of having his working years coincide with an era of strong unionism and, relatedly, a robust middle class.

His story offers a layman's entry point into the complex issue of teacher compensation and pension reform and how it relates to broader economic and demographic trends. His story—the quintessential Baby Boomer story—presents a sharp set of contrasts to the story of teachers' lives in 2016.

Career expectations   A compensation system with an end-loaded pension was ideal in the era when a career was defined as a decades-long relationship with one employer. This system does not work in the world in which the average worker stays at a job for 4.4 years.[3]

In urban teaching, where thousands of newer teachers are subject to layoffs annually, the churn is even more intense.

Middle-class purchasing power   In 1973 at the end of his fourth year of teaching, my dad got a mortgage for a $34,000 home (the precise median home price in America that year) based on his $11,000+ annual income. His mortgage fit squarely into the "three times annual income" calculation that banks use in determining how much home a borrower can afford. By comparison, fourth-year teachers in America today cannot consider a home priced at the national median of $242,300.[4]

Life expectancy   When Baby Boomers began entering the workforce in the late 1960s, the average American lived for 69.7 years. Today, the average US resident can expect to live a decade longer (to 79.3),[5] at a minimum tripling his or her "retirement" years.

With a few decades of historical perspective, we can see two points clearly: the first is how good a teacher's total compensation was a generation ago; the second is how broken the system is becoming now. A teacher entering the classroom today benefits far less from the early stability and purchasing power of his career choice than a teacher in 1969. And even without a degree in actuarial math, it is obvious that retirement benefits become unsustainable when making an extra ten years of payments per average recipient.

Moreover, it is stunning how well the total compensation package for a teacher lined up with workers' priorities of the day: job stability, a middle-class lifestyle, and a secure retirement that one dared hope would have a long horizon. In fact, I feel both frustrated and jealous that those former pillars of the American Dream have crumbled, even from our lexicon of aspiration, just a generation later.

Where do we begin on the path to building a pension system that doesn't further shortchange Millennials?

I argue that we should start with a new set of givens. If job mobility is a given, how can a pension system work with, rather than against, that reality? If teachers need more cash earlier in their careers to get a foothold in the middle class, what are the implications for the overall structure of compensation? If those entering the classroom today will comfortably live into their eighties, what promises are we prepared to make now and keep through 2070?

I'm saddened that almost any change to the pension system will result in a smaller package going forward. Perhaps that is the reason teachers have not been proactive in redefining pensions and compensation more broadly. The data show that this inaction is costing the profession. Since 2008, teachers in twenty-one states have found themselves with an increase in required contributions while facing reduced benefits. This disproportionately affects newer cohorts of teachers.[6]

An immediate step must be to listen carefully to those teachers who are early in their careers today. As a starting point, I offer the ideas of Jacob Pactor, an educator from Indianapolis:

> Unions should help retain [newer] teachers by fixing voluntary retirement plans. Until I've taught for fifteen years in my current district, I'm not vested in a retirement plan. That structure disincentivizes teachers of my generation from staying. Teachers should vest based on classroom performance. Unions can lead on this and incentivize effective teachers to stay by linking voluntary retirement plan contributions to classroom performance. This would encourage more effective teachers to stay in the classroom longer.
>
> Teachers evaluated as highly effective should vest immediately with a higher percentage and with the opportunity for higher matching contributions. If McDonald's can do it with a "supersized 401(k) match," so can schools. Those matching contributions should be extended to all teachers, but at tiered levels: for example, highly effective teachers receive a 5 percent match of their pay; effective teachers receive 3 percent; and teachers deemed ineffective lose their district's matching opportunity until they improve.

I'm sure that Jacob's words sound nothing like what my dad's would have in the early 1970s. Those generational tensions are natural and important to bring to the surface. My dad is all set. If we're going to solve the pension crisis for the long term and in the best interest of teachers, more Millennials like Jacob need to enter the conversation.

Key Takeaways

☐ Many of us share an implicit belief that there could be One Best System for education in the United States.

☐ In fact, the education system reflects a continual process of making trade-offs that benefit certain participants more than others.

☐ Making trade-offs is a hallmark of policymaking, and advocates should recognize that decision makers are trained to think in terms of trade-offs.

☐ Teachers' unions would benefit from internal conversations about generational differences and differences in performance because these conversations are taking place among policymakers.

Notes

1. Even the new federal law, the Every Student Succeeds Act, is an acknowledgment of the federal overreach toward national uniformity of policy represented by NCLB, as it returns much more decision-making power to states and districts.
2. Greg Toppo and Paul Overberg, "Fewer Than Half of Teachers Now Covered by Unions," *USA Today,* February 10, 2015, http://www.usatoday.com/story/news/nation/2015/02/10/teacher-unions-fewer-half/23195433/.
3. Jeanne Meister, "The Future of Work: Job-Hopping is the 'New Normal' for Millennials," *Forbes,* August 14, 2012, https://www.forbes.com/sites/jeannemeister/2012/08/14/the-future-of-work-job-hopping-is-the-new-normal-for-millennials/#5036c91813b8.
4. US Census Bureau, "Median and Average Sales Prices of New Homes Sold in the United States" (n.d.), http://www.census.gov/const/uspricemon.pdf.
5. National Center for Health Statistics, "Life Expectancy" (March 17, 2017), https://www.cdc.gov/nchs/fastats/life-expectancy.htm.
6. Kathryn M. Doherty, Sandi Jacobs, and Trisha M. Madden, *No One Benefits: How Teacher Pension Systems Are Failing BOTH Teachers and Taxpayers* (Washington, DC: National Center for Teacher Quality, 2013).

CHAPTER · **N I N E**

Power

LESSON

If You're Not at the Table, You're on the Menu

This chapter focuses on power dynamics. At this point in the book, you may be able to see the principles of equity, resource scarcity, and accountability at play in decision making in a way you haven't in the past. At the same time, anyone who's watched *House of Cards* knows that policymaking is not simply an exercise in sharpening one's point of view on these topics and pursuing a pure agenda that serves kids in schools. Politics also come into play. Individuals, their relationships with one another, the power dynamics of groups, and the numbers of people associated with a particular issue all matter tremendously.

Pick the right size issue, the right audience, and the right outcome goal for the change you want to see.

As a focal point for the lessons of this section, I describe the start and end of a major partnership between Teach Plus and the National Education Association to engage early-career teachers in their unions. It serves as an illustration of the different approaches teachers can take to advocacy depending on the relative amount of power they have as a group. From there, we home in on how to pick the right size issue, the right audience, and the right outcome goal for the change you want to see.

The Power of Policymakers and the Power of Teachers

If there is no such thing as one best policy for all, it is inevitable that the question of which policies get adopted will be a contested one. In a world where it is impossible to assess what policy will play out in the best way for kids, those with greater power tend to have an outsize role in setting the agenda. In a fundamental way, district, state, and federal leaders have power because they control school budgets and the laws governing schools.

As a counterweight to that power, especially over the last fifty years, teachers have found their own strength in organizing as a collective. Unions and/or professional associations of teachers exist in all fifty states. However, little more than half of states guarantee teachers collective bargaining rights by law.[1]

Over the past decade, organizations like Teach Plus have created new forums for educators to connect and have a voice. Just like unions, who control neither the purse strings nor the rules, this next generation of teacher organizing will be powerful only if its numbers grow rapidly, creating a force for decision makers to reckon with.

One of the questions insurgent groups like ours must wrestle with is whether to pursue change from outside the traditional unions (by advancing an agenda that is different from the union's) or whether to work with the unions to help facilitate change from within. We have done both. The next section discusses an example of working to change the union from within.

Changing the Profession from within the Union

I have one favorite project that we've done at Teach Plus. That's a little bit like saying you have a favorite child—completely inappropriate. Each project has involved incredible teachers seeking to accomplish something important. But my favorite was working directly with the NEA, even though this project ultimately came to an end that disappointed me. There were a number of important ways in which this project was a success and, in one important way, a failure. At its essence, our work with the NEA is a story of power dynamics.

At the end of 2012, Teach Plus released a report on generational differences in the teaching profession. It was called *Great Expectations: Teachers' Views on Elevating the Profession.*[2] The study documented the findings from a survey of over one thousand teachers nationally; approximately half of the respondents had more than ten years' teaching experience, and the other half had less than ten years' experience. The results showed wide generational gaps in teacher perspectives on certain issues and shared beliefs across generations on other issues (Summarized in Figure 9.1). For example, on the question of whether growth in student learning should be part of a teacher's evaluation, a majority of veteran teachers disagreed (56 percent), whereas only 26 percent of newer teachers disagreed—a 30 percentage point difference between generations.

The study resulted in my being invited to conduct a briefing for a number of senior leaders at the NEA, including then president Dennis Van Roekel.

Figure 9.1   Areas of Agreement and Disagreement across Different Generations of Teachers

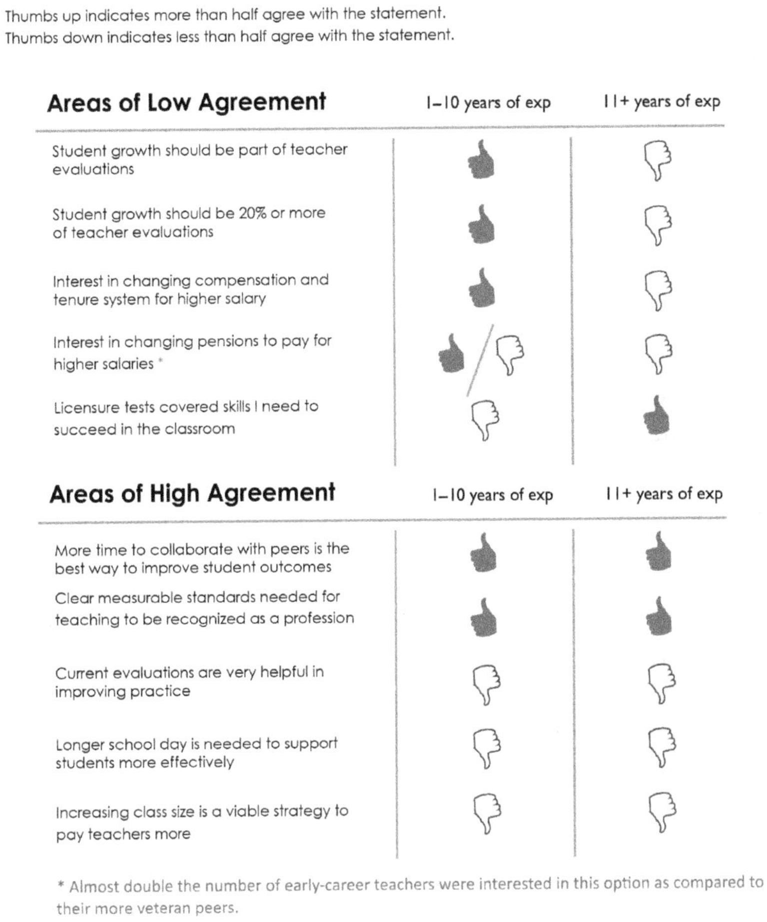

Thumbs up indicates more than half agree with the statement.
Thumbs down indicates less than half agree with the statement.

Areas of Low Agreement

	1–10 years of exp	11+ years of exp
Student growth should be part of teacher evaluations	👍	👎
Student growth should be 20% or more of teacher evaluations	👍	👎
Interest in changing compensation and tenure system for higher salary	👍	👎
Interest in changing pensions to pay for higher salaries *	👍/👎	👎
Licensure tests covered skills I need to succeed in the classroom	👎	👍

Areas of High Agreement

	1–10 years of exp	11+ years of exp
More time to collaborate with peers is the best way to improve student outcomes	👍	👍
Clear measurable standards needed for teaching to be recognized as a profession	👍	👍
Current evaluations are very helpful in improving practice	👎	👎
Longer school day is needed to support students more effectively	👎	👎
Increasing class size is a viable strategy to pay teachers more	👎	👎

* Almost double the number of early-career teachers were interested in this option as compared to their more veteran peers.

Dennis impressed me with how forward thinking he was about wanting to attract the active participation of greater numbers of young teachers to the union. At the same time, he acknowledged that it was hard for the union to do this attracting on its own, both because "shaking things up" was slow in a multimillion-member bureaucracy and because the interests of new teachers were sometimes at odds of those who had "waited their turn" and risen to power after decades of service. To him, outside assistance from us could help drive a better conversation internally.

We decided to launch a national policy fellowship in partnership with the NEA on the topic of the "next generation of unions." I felt that this was the role we were always meant to play. We hired a rock-star twenty-something union president named Arielle Zurzolo (who came from the Green Dot Schools in California) to lead the work. By the next summer, we had selected fifty-three teachers from around the country, all of whom had between three and ten years' classroom experience, to participate in the fellowship.

We brought them together three times in Washington DC for a long weekend of training and held monthly online meetings in between. They met with Dennis and innovative union presidents from around the country, such as Paul Toner from Massachusetts and Carrie Dallman from Colorado. They also met in person with some of the top education policy-makers in the country, including secretary of education Arne Duncan and US congressman George Miller (D-CA).

Their commitment to finding a way to be a "new voice" within the union was as high as it could be. There was a palpable feeling of collective energy that only grew over the year of the project. But make no mistake, that energy was fueled by frustration that the current union wasn't living up to its potential and wasn't finding enough ways to tap into the wisdom of people entering teaching in the new millennium. This was a group of problem solvers and "doers."

When we first met together as a group, Michaela Kovacs, a teacher from Colorado, described a vision of "the club she'd want to join," which would be led by excellent, expert teachers and would be focused, first and foremost, on helping teachers get better at serving students. That was what the union teachers were looking for. Ultimately, they added detail to their vision by studying budgets and contracts and how the union had evolved historically. On May 20, 2014, they released their recommendations at an event at the NEA headquarters in Washington DC.

Their report was called *Rock the Union: An Action Plan to Engage Early Career Teachers and Elevate the Profession.* Their recommendations included the following:

- A specific budgetary shift toward improving teaching and learning and away from "defensive unionism"
- Greater leadership pathways programs for excellent teachers within the union

- Three specific ways to define a space for early-career teachers within existing NEA governance structures

Finally, they sought to create a Rock the Union campaign within the NEA to engage and inform early-career teachers.

The action plan that the report laid out was pure awesomeness, start to finish. It was desperately needed, and these were the right teachers to lead it! Unfortunately, the plan never made it out of the NEA headquarters, except physically in the hands of the participating teachers.

We originally had a two-part plan: first an internal release to NEA higher-ups; second, a public release with NEA leaders and the teachers side by side. Two weeks after the internal release, a new NEA president was elected, along with a number of new executive board members. They had other priority issues and decided that Rock the Union would not go any further as a national initiative. The teachers were able to advance the recommendations locally using our materials, but Teach Plus was asked to take the report down from its website.

That plan was the best thing I've ever been a part of professionally. I really believe it is the right North Star for the profession over the next decade. But only about two hundred people on earth have ever laid eyes on it.

The NEA has three million members. I had been sure that our group was playing a role in changing the teaching profession. And then we were effectively uninvited from the table. Changes to who is in power have consequences for the agenda, and this change resulted in a setback for our work.

Where does Rock the Union stand now?

Non-Sellout Strategies for Rocking Your Union

Although Rock the Union did not become a major national initiative of the NEA, the teachers are continuing to grow it in local, grassroots ways. Most prominently, Colorado teachers, with a grant from the NEA Foundation, have launched a teacher-led professional development network, aligned to the first recommendation of the report, to serve hundreds of teachers over a three-year period.

The data from the first year are in and speak to the power of the work. Of the participating teachers, 100 percent agreed that "their

(continued)

local association should continue to focus on a new priority of offering teacher-led professional development," and 98.5 percent reported incorporating "new strategies or practices into their classroom over the past 5 weeks." In the words of one of the teacher leaders: "This is the best thing I can possibly think of for the profession. The feedback was overwhelmingly positive from participants. Everyone wins. Teachers are given the opportunity to lead and are paid well for their efforts. Participants receive graduate credit in an environment that they can learn from and with their colleagues. This is the best thing I have ever been a part of in my experience teaching for the last eight years."

In addition, almost all of the teachers who started the NEA fellowship not holding a union leadership role have been elected to union leadership roles. Many teachers have taken up the mantle of enacting local programs that flow from the report's push for increased teacher leadership. The following is a small sample of what the fellows have gone on to do:

- Matthew Courtney founded the Bluegrass Center for Teacher Quality to advance teacher-led professional development in Kentucky.
- Ellyn Metcalf launched the Total Teacher Project, which has trained teachers from four New England states in leadership skills.
- Lisa Alva ran in 2017 for a seat on the Los Angeles Unified Board to bring greater teacher voice to decision-making in the district.

These teachers are building a movement (and their own leadership in that movement) that will be ready to connect back with the national NEA leaders at some point that I am hopeful will come again in the future.

Advocating from a Position of Power: Forging Ahead

The story I've told here is a jumping-off point for a few lessons in how you as an advocate can be most effective when the power dynamic is on your side (discussed in this section), and what actions to take when your idea, group, or party is not in power (discussed in the next section).

When the power dynamic favors you:

1. **Move quickly.** An important part of having power is recognizing that it won't last, and acting while you can. The NEA fellows convened as a group for the first time in mid-October and presented a polished twenty-eight-page report in mid-May of the next year, a mere seven months later. In that time, they did an exhausting amount of work: getting to know and build trust with one another, studying research and best practices from around the country, requesting and analyzing NEA budgets, coming to consensus on ideas, and writing and editing the report. Any one of them could have argued that they needed more time, but they seized the moment they had.

2. **Be specific in your vision.** It is not enough to say, "There should be more opportunities for career growth in teaching." The fellows were extremely detailed in their description of the role the NEA could play. They answered such questions as "How much money should be spent?" and "What parts of the overall NEA budget should grow and shrink accordingly? And by how much?" They surveyed hundreds of their peers to be able to share data on the percentage of early-career teachers who aspire to hybrid roles that couple part-time classroom teaching with part-time leadership.

3. **Communicate with everyone.** To create a plan that can be enacted, it is necessary to attend to differences in opinion among the people who would be affected by the plan. Too often, people plan in an echo chamber where one set of ideas is favored. Ultimately, those plans meet heavy resistance in implementation. The time between October and May was a time when fellows both talked and listened. They talked up their basic ideas in their home districts and heard both positive and negative feedback. This helped them sharpen certain parts of the plan and determine which parts to emphasize and which to leave on the cutting-room floor. As you move into your own advocacy, you'll have conversations with at least four types of people, and they all have a purpose:

   a. **Undiscovered evangelists.** Conversations bring new people into fighting for the cause by giving them an entry point to understanding the issue, and helping them recognize what it would take to make a change and see how their actions could matter.

b. **On-the-fence converts.** There are some people who may start out as neutral toward your idea. Talking with them—both the act of taking the time and the new information provided—may bring them off the fence and into your camp.

c. **The neutralized.** There were many veteran educators who were skeptical about newer teachers being awarded a prestigious fellowship and the access to decision making that came with it. They started out as unlikely to support any recommendations the fellows came up with. However, as the veterans got to know the fellows, many were won over by their commitment to their union and their passion for improving it.

d. **Fixed foes.** It is not possible to win everyone over. It is better to know who opposes your ideas and why—and to strategize with that knowledge in mind—than to ignore them and hope for the best later.

4. **Look for third-way solutions.** In response to the spectrum of feedback on their ideas, the fellows made some adjustments designed to allow a greater portion of NEA leaders to be supportive of their plan. Sometimes language is the way to thread the needle between different perspectives, as the fellows learned. Their initial draft laid out their vision for a "performance-driven profession" in which high-performing teachers had access to differentiated compensation and career pathways. They received feedback that the phrase *performance-driven* evoked a negative connection to *test-based* and would alienate too many existing leaders. The fellows decided to keep all of the elements of their vision the same, but instead to label them as elements of a "quality-driven profession." The details of the plan were untouched, but the fellows no longer risked losing their audience due to the semantics of the label they chose.

5. **Expect (demand) more.** One of the guest speakers who met with the fellows shortly before their report release was Maddie Fennell,

former Nebraska Teacher of the Year. She reminded the group that with reports like theirs, leaders often implement one among a series of recommendations and tell the group they listened and took action. "If the NEA just took one step to better engage early-career teachers, would that be enough?" she asked. Of course, the group's answer was no. They clarified that they saw the multiple recommendations as interdependent and that all were needed. Maddie's message was for them to hold leaders accountable for implementing all the recommendations, not just some.

6. **Build a legacy.** The skills the fellows developed and the starting point they established for forging the work locally allowed the ideas to continue in various forms after the national partnership with NEA ended. The work that Matthew, Ellyn, Michaela, and their colleagues started locally continues several years later.

Advocating with Limited Political Power: Building the Movement

What do you do when your group, issue, or party is not in power? For many teachers, especially those who teach vulnerable low-income or undocumented students, the election of President Trump meant a transition to being squarely in the "out-of-power" camp. That is not a reason to give up fighting for your students. It is cause to set new expectations, grow your base, and be strategic about moving toward a better future. Loss of power doesn't mean you cannot accomplish change; it only means that you're likely to find it harder and slower. Perseverance matters.

> If you want to be successful in policy and advocacy, you need to be able to find an open window when the door is closed.

When the power dynamic does not favor you:

1. **Don't give up, but learn patience.** It is important to acknowledge that you are pushing into a headwind and expect the pace of progress

to slow accordingly. If people have the expectation—implicit or explicit—that progress will continue at the same pace as when you were in power, they will become frustrated and disengaged.

2. **Recognize that your constituency is still there, but needs a new plan.** When our fellows were working with NEA leaders, they were working with a mix of people—some of whom were excited about the work and some of whom were skeptical. When the partnership ended, there were probably just as many people who were disappointed as there were people who wanted to see it end. There was still a constituency within the union that wanted to see changes made for newer teachers, but they needed a different plan for a different administration.

   There are parallels to the 2016 presidential election. The Democrats lost. But that does not mean that fewer people believe in the principles of the Democratic Party. Nor does it mean that there isn't important work for Democrats to do over the next four years. What it means is that they need to throw out the playbook that got them to this point and start operating from a new one. The need for a new plan is a leadership opportunity.

3. **Find a window when the door is closed.** One of my mentors, former Massachusetts secretary of education Paul Reville, always described himself as an entrepreneur when the rest of the world would call him a policy expert. He would say that if you want to be successful in policy and advocacy, you need to be able to find an open window when the door is closed. You need to find a novel entry point to getting attention for an issue that you care about. In essence, you have to be an entrepreneur.

   In the cases of Matthew, Ellyn, and Michaela, they were able to find open windows in their states to carry on good work when the door was closed at the national level.

4. **Get creative to build support.** Related to the last point, this is the moment to figure out new ways to tell the story of your issue. This is the moment to study whether you are asking the right questions. It is a time to seek out new data to better understand the nature of your problem and communicate it. It is an opportunity to look for new people to engage in your cause.

Recall how the Teach Plus partnership with the NEA began. New data about how less experienced teachers had a different stance on many key issues than veteran teachers caught the interest of the NEA president. These new data allowed a group that felt relatively weak in terms of power (newer teachers) to get a forum with the top brass.

5. **Pick your battles (and fight them).** Our partnership with the national office of the NEA ended amicably, with both organizations recognizing that the next stage of the work could flourish at the state and local levels. There was no "battle" as the new leadership came into power and decided to place emphasis on different issues.

However, I would be remiss if I did not acknowledge the need to occasionally take on a major advocacy fight with limited political power. When your issue or group is weak in power, it is generally a time to look for compromise in the interest of maintaining a seat at the decision-making table. However, it is important not to compromise on your core beliefs.

For those of us who see education as a civil rights issue and see our role as protecting and ensuring the success of our nation's most vulnerable students, the Trump presidency is cause for serious concern. It will be important for communities of teachers, through unions and other vehicles, to draw and defend lines in the sand on such issues as federal funding for poor students.

Action Steps for Building Power

- Meet one-on-one with decision makers
- Create and circulate petitions
- Create a coalition of groups with similar interests (for example, a PTA and a union)
- Do writing and research (for example, blog posts, letters to the editor, policy memos)
- Testify before a decision-making body (for example, a school committee)

Finding the Sweet Spot for Effective Advocacy

At this point, you might say: I know that there are things I would like to change, and I know where I stand in terms of relative power, but I'm not clear on what to do next.

A common tactic for community organizers who are attempting large-scale change is to engage in a root cause analysis. Think of root cause analysis in terms of a tree. When a tree is sick, you see the manifestation of the sickness above ground in dying leaves or falling branches. Yet the cause is buried under the visible landscape, at the roots.

Think about the major problems we see in US education. One that is visible in every state is the achievement gap between White and Asian students and Black and Latino students. This problem has deep roots, including the history of race relations in the United States, poverty, and the way the housing market and education funding are structured. However, "closing the achievement gap" is such a big problem, with so many overlapping reasons for its existence, that it is difficult to figure out how to take action at the policy level. Finding the sweet spot for action means picking one issue within the larger problem. Refer to Table 9.1 for a summary of how problems and issues differ.

The job of an advocate is to find the sweet spot in which a concrete change can be made and have an immediate impact on a facet of the

Table 9.1 Characteristics of Problems versus Characteristics of Issues

Problems . . .	Issues . . .
Are vast and broad	Are immediate
Are vague	Are specific
Are multifaceted	Are focused
Are overwhelming	Are winnable (and losable)
Result from many, overlapping causes	Have a clear cause
Are influenced by many people's decisions, at varying levels, across time	Have clear decision makers
Defeat and discourage would-be advocates	Give advocates a goal to organize around
Do not have clear policy levers	Have tangible levers for change

problem. The sweet spot is the place where a person or group can be held accountable for enacting a change. By tackling concrete issues, we can address problems in an actionable way. For example, in the case of tackling the achievement gap, the sweet spot we focus on at Teach Plus is ensuring that students of color get improved access to high-quality teachers.

To recap:

Problems are really big and hard to tackle. People tend to get stuck here.

Root causes are deep and operate at a societal level.

Issues are concrete and can empower people to act.

The sweet spot is found at the **issue** level where teachers and other advocates can be mobilized toward a defined end.

The NEA work described earlier in the chapter can be analyzed in terms of problems, root causes, and finding a sweet spot. The big problem—I bet you've lamented this with your colleagues—is the status of the teaching profession. How can we elevate teaching to keep great people in the profession? The roots of this problem are deep. They include (1) the history of teaching as a field for women and people of color, (2) the lack of a specific knowledge base that all teachers share, and (3) weakening power of unions in the United States. The sweet spot we identified was around strengthening the union role in creating a dynamic career where teachers can be empowered leaders while continuing to work with students.

Identifying the sweet spot for your issue allows you to move from generic to specific in terms of the change you seek. You may wish to fix the problem—that is, the current status of the teaching profession. You can't actually do anything toward that end until you have identified

1. A specific policy you seek to have added or changed

2. A specific audience for your advocacy

For example, the fellows sought changes to the budget (and governance) as the way to change policy on their issue (point 1) and identified the NEA president as the decision maker to target (point 2).

To get to specifics, you'll need to research what rules are currently in place on your issue and who is responsible for them. Suppose, for example, that you want to see changes to special education in your school. Start by looking into what is in your teacher's contract that relates to the issue. What are other related district policies? What are some of the state and federal laws that apply?

Knowing something is "law" is not the same as knowing what the state law actually says. There has been plenty of research showing that people assume that certain routine practices in their schools are instantiated in their contracts or in state law when, in fact, they are not. There may be flexibility to operate differently, and people are simply not taking advantage of it.[3] You can't know what you want to change until you know exactly what exists.

Once you have done your homework on existing policy, you'll need to determine whom you will need to influence to make a change. If it is a state-level issue, your path forward might be through the state legislature, or it might be through your state's board of education or through an official at the department of education. There are right and wrong policymakers to approach on every issue.

A good rule of thumb for holding yourself accountable as you begin to take action on your sweet spot is the idea of a two-by-two matrix. As an activity for your group during its first month, figure out at least **two** major policies (at any level of the system) on the issue and **two** key decision makers on the issue. If you can get to that level of specificity, you'll feel the momentum building, giving you both direction and forward movement.

Key Takeaways

☐ Education is a political issue, and power dynamics are inescapable.

☐ Advocates should use different playbooks depending on whether they are in a position of power or not.

☐ Gaining traction on solving a problem involves finding the sweet spot for action.

☐ Once you've identified the sweet spot, the next steps are to get clear on what specific policies stand in the way of the future you envision and who are the key decision makers to target.

Notes

1. Alexander Russo, "Maps: Which States Have Collective Bargaining?" *This Week in Education,* February 22, 2011, http://scholasticadministrator.typepad.com/thisweekineducation/2011/02/maps-which-states-have-collective-bargaining.html#.WesUoiMrIzU.
2. Teach Plus, *Great Expectations: Teachers' Views on Elevating the Profession* (2012), http://www.teachplus.org/sites/default/files/publication/pdf/great_expectations.pdf.
3. Frederick M. Hess, *The Cage-Busting Teacher* (Cambridge, MA: Harvard Education Press, 2014).

Taking Action

LESSON
Your Story Has to Meet the Moment

W hat do Hurricane Katrina and the 2008 collapse of the US financial market have in common?
What do they have to do with education?
What was the catalyst for Race to the Top?
What do any of these things have to do with you as an advocate?
Once you understand the education system that you are trying to influence, you need a plan of action. That plan needs to be connected to you as a leader (even if you don't feel ready to be a leader or comfortable in that role), and it needs to be connected to the larger social context of the moment. In this, the final chapter of the book, we'll walk through the steps of building an advocacy plan, and analyze examples of how others successfully seized the moment to bring about change.

The framework for this chapter comes from the work of Harvard professor Marshall Ganz, who worked alongside Caesar Chavez organizing farmworkers in California in the 1960s. Ganz codified the practices of effective community organizing in ways that are applicable to education advocacy. He orients community organizing around storytelling and breaks effective "public narrative" into three elements:

- **A story of self:** how you came to be the person you are.
- **A story of us:** how your constituency, community, organization, came to be the people they are; and
- **A story of now:** the challenge this community now faces, the choices it must make and the outcomes to which "we" can aspire.[1]

Over the course of this chapter, we will explore how to develop our stories and why it matters. What this introduction to the three elements makes clear is that *individuals and their personal stories matter* in catalyzing change, and *the particular moment in history matters* to the likelihood of success. Policy change is not effected in a vacuum. It rarely takes off from a standing start.

For our purposes here, we will start with the role of "now" in advocacy. To do so, it's time to revisit the questions that opened the chapter.

Connecting "the Now" and Your Cause: Entry Points and Galvanizing Moments

Very often, societal forces push the state legislature, local school board, or other decision-making body to take action or devote resources to something new. The people who become influential are those who can recognize a moment of crisis (or a moment of transition or a moment of uncertainty) and insert their idea for change as part of the solution. Remember: helping those in power solve *their* problems is the fastest way to solving yours. If policymakers are being pushed by the moment to act and you have a viable solution, you will get heard. Moments of crisis represent **entry points** that can amplify attention to your issue.

Recall from chapter 9 that influencers are entrepreneurs. The best advocates see the landscape in the state, anticipate issues before they are completely clear to others, and bring viable solutions to the conversation. They can take advantage of uncertainty rather than run from it. Right now, I imagine you might be skeptical that you could recognize an entry point if you saw one. I want to break down a couple of crises that you inevitably watched for weeks on the news as they occurred. At the time, you may not have been thinking about their implications for education, but the discussion here will help you connect the dots between important moments in the larger environment and their implications for spurring changes in education policy.

Two Tectonic Shifts in Education, and "the Now" That Created Them

In the following descriptions, you'll see the entry points for change that people capitalized on. These entry points can also be understood as **galvanizing moments**. That is, they were moments when a problem captured the attention of the larger public, and the larger public pressed leaders for solutions. Leaders were forced to develop new solutions in real time in response to broad public pressure for action. Under normal circumstances, many in leadership positions would prefer inertia to the possible controversy of standing up for a new idea. The galvanizing moment counteracts inertia and forces leaders toward action and new ideas.

Hurricane Katrina and Charter Expansion in New Orleans

Advocacy for charter schools has been a growing movement within the education sector for almost three decades. In that time, the number of students (and parents) served by charters has risen steadily, though unevenly. Never has the charter sector grown as quickly as in New Orleans as a direct response to Hurricane Katrina. In moment of crisis, when most schools in the previously failing district were destroyed, charter advocates moved quickly, presenting massive expansion of charter schools as a mechanism to solve a variety of pressing problems. Charter schools could help the district garner new federal and philanthropic dollars for the recovery, spur schools to reopen faster, draw new teaching and administrative talent to the city, and improve test scores.

> What happened to the New Orleans public schools following the tragic levee breeches after Hurricane Katrina is truly unprecedented. Within the span of one year, all public-school employees were fired, the teacher contract expired and was not replaced, and most attendance zones were eliminated. The state took control of almost all public schools and began holding them to relatively strict standards of academic achievement. Over time, the state turned all the schools under its authority over to charter management organizations (CMOs) that, in turn, dramatically reshaped the teacher workforce.
>
> A few states and districts nationally have experimented with one or two of these reforms; many states have increased the number of charter schools, for example. But no city had gone as far on any one of these dimensions or considered trying all of them at once. New Orleans essentially erased its traditional school district and started over. In the process, the city has provided the first direct test of an alternative to the system that has dominated American public education for more than a century.[2]

In terms of raising student achievement, especially among disadvantaged students, New Orleans has been heralded as a success. Student scores on state tests rose significantly, and much faster than for similar students, and high school graduation rates rose by 10 percent. Critics, though, cite that these improvements came at the expense of the pre-Katrina work-force, which was largely replaced, and the broader contract protections that existed with a unionized workforce.

For students of policy, it is instructive to view the post-Katrina schools in New Orleans through the lens of the galvanizing moment. A natural disaster unrelated to school reform catalyzed the type of dramatic trans-formation that can rarely occur in democratically controlled schools where compromise and "tinkering" are the norm, where opposing "sides" keep one another in check but also inhibit big changes. There was a moment in time when help was needed (an entry point), and there was a particular point of view on how to help that won the day. People were there to shape the direction of the response and turn a crisis in the physical world into a revolution in the world of school choice.

The 2008 Financial Collapse and Race to the Top

Following the financial collapse of late 2008, one of President Obama's first major acts as president was to initiate the American Recovery and Reinvestment Act (ARRA), a roughly $800 billion stimulus package to stem job losses and provide relief to states from the recession. Ensuring that schools were not eviscerated was a major priority, budgeted at approx-imately $100 billion. Within that $100 billion (which was largely distrib-uted in noncompetitive block grants) was the $4.35 billion Race to the Top program.

Race to the Top was a competitive grant program that used the funds available in a crisis moment as an incentive for states and districts to make changes to their local policies. It created a significant financial incentive for states to align their policies with the priorities of the federal government, thus using limited federal dollars to leverage far greater resources and man-power for education reform in fifty states. Signature priorities of the com-petition included "improving teacher and principal effectiveness based on performance," "developing and adopting common standards," and expand-ing charter schools.

Race to the Top motivated a tremendous amount of state activity aimed at winning the dollars by adjusting policy to better fit the Race to the Top criteria. Forty states applied for funds (only eleven received them), and, in the process of enhancing the competitiveness of their applications, at least thirty-two states passed new laws related to Race to the Top issues.

In his best seller *Class Warfare: Inside the Fight to Fix America's Schools,* Steven Brill describes how a few key influencers steered the education portion of ARRA away from the expected block grants to districts toward significant dollars for a competition that rewarded innovation. Soon after President Obama was elected, a handful of education leaders were posed the question, "If you guys got, say, $100 billion for education as part of the [stimulus] package, could you use it to move some of Obama's reform ideas?"[3] That was a moment of opportunity for people who already had knowledge of what was working best for students across the country. Of course, most of the dollars were sent in block grants, but the $4.35 billion that was allocated to Race to the Top generated the most reform activity, controversy, and change.

Non-Sellout Strategy: Teachers Meeting Their Galvanizing Moment

At this point, you're probably convinced that larger forces can lead to significant and almost immediate shifts in education policy. But you're probably also skeptical that as a teacher, you could be anything but a recipient of those new policies—policies that were rushed in their conception and whose problems only become clear as they hit your classroom, at that.

Recall from chapter 5 the story of Boston teachers who developed a proposal to ensure that the highest-need students had better access to excellent teaching. It was a teacher-developed idea for advancing a team-based approach to improving low-performing schools. Participating schools could recruit or "promote from within" excellent, experienced teachers who had a track record of strong student growth in urban schools. Teacher leaders received training and additional compensation to support their peers.

You may have noted when you read the passage in chapter 5 that the teachers proposed their idea in early 2009, but that it didn't move forward for more than a year.

(continued)

The Boston group was the first cohort of policy fellows, and we held our first big event to release the proposal. Dr. Carol Johnson, then superintendent of the Boston Public Schools, spoke at the event and reflected positively on the proposal after the teachers presented it. Several union leaders, school committee members, and other influencers were in the crowd of about 150, who gave it a positive reception.

And then the proposal sat.

And sat.

And sat.

I remember these months because I was leading the teachers, and they were looking to me for help. Could Teach Plus successfully help teachers "have a voice," only to then fail to have that voice heard in a way that mattered in terms of effecting changes that would benefit schools? Ugh. That was not what any of us was going for.

Through lots of meetings with district and union leaders and the mayor's office, the simple policy maxim came to life: policy rarely changes from a standing start. Leaders liked the idea, but did not have significant impetus to launch a new program that would benefit some schools and not others. (Recall that there are always winners and losers in a change in district policy.) This proposal would be controversial in that it would introduce differentiated pay for teachers and concentrate greater resources in some schools over others.

In addition, of course, was the fact that it would be expensive. Teacher leader stipends would need to be substantial, given the added work. Recruitment, selection, and training would raise the price tag further.

The new year came, and it had been almost ten months since the proposal was released to great fanfare and then relegated to the proverbial shelf. In January 2010, however, the fate of the proposal changed, but not through the efforts of the teachers. Race to the Top fever had spread to the Massachusetts legislature. Our state, like most others, wanted to pass at least one major new law as evidence of its commitment to implementing the Race to the Top principles. On January 18 of that year, an omnibus bill known as An Act Relative to the Achievement Gap was signed into law. One of its central areas of focus was aggressive intervention in persistently low-performing schools. One strategy that the law would force in certain schools was dismissal of half of the teaching staff.

Often, the galvanizing moment does not come in a form that you'd like. Just as no one wanted Hurricane Katrina or the financial collapse, most teachers didn't like the dismissal provision. What lawmakers failed to recognize in their new law was that the dismissal of half of the faculty at a low-performing school was likely to result in that school being unable to attract the type of experienced, high-performing teachers who would be needed for the school to improve. It was most likely that the vacancies would be filled by brand-new teachers who hadn't figured out how to land in more stable schools, perpetuating the cycle of low performance.

What the schools needed was an aggressive strategy to attract some of the district's best teachers to these schools. The teachers relaunched conversations with leaders about their proposal, and this time the leaders were ready to act. The teachers' idea was now helping leaders, forced to implement a new law, solve their problems.

Even as some union members picketed against the dismissal of teachers from the targeted schools, they agreed to try the teacher-developed proposal. It came to life in three Boston schools as T3 (Turnaround Teacher Teams), and—seven years later—it has served thousands of students in several cities across the country. The teachers had found their moment.

Connecting "the Now" and Your Story

In the case of getting T3 off the ground and into schools, the messenger mattered. Who better to communicate the conditions under which historically low-performing schools could attract strong, experienced teachers than strong, experienced teachers themselves?

Telling your story is a way of building power and asserting

Combining the how and why is the path-to action and mobilization.

yourself as a leader. Stories connect us to the *why* of a movement or change effort. In the case of T3, the teachers had a clear plan; that is, they had a plan for *how* to enact a change. Their stories provided a second necessary element of leadership, the *why*. The *why* refers to what motivates you. Why are you passionate about this issue? The way you describe your motivation can in turn motivate others. Strong advocates communicate from both the head (articulating the *how*) and the heart (articulating the *why*). Combining the how and why is the path to action and mobilization.

Stories allow others to step into your shoes, and give them a reason to follow you. In this case, the teachers had compelling stories of individual students whose needs were not being met, as well as stories of their own experiences, hopes, and aspirations. Embedded in their narratives were lessons about the choices the district had made to date and possibilities for its future. Emotion influences values, and values influence action.

Stories have sticking power. They help listeners get in touch with their values and question whether the choices they are making align to those values. It is ideal to be able to pair your unique experience with a larger data set of teachers who share your beliefs. But research shows that your audience is more likely to remember the story than they are the data. Stories and data complement each other as advocacy tools.

Good stories have a beginning, middle, and end. Ganz lays this out clearly:

> A good public story is drawn from the series of choice points that have structured the "plot" of your life—the **challenges** you faced, **choices** you made, and **outcomes you experienced**
>
> **Challenge:** Why did you feel it was a challenge? What was so challenging about it? Why was it *your* challenge?
> **Choice:** Why did you make the choice you did? Where did you get the courage—or not? Where did you get the hope—or not? How did it feel?
> **Outcome:** How did the outcome feel? Why did it feel that way? What did it teach you? What do you want to teach us? How do you want us to feel?[4]

Stories have the power to transform stagnation to motivation (Figure 10.1) and to inspire a belief in YCMAD—*You can make a difference.*

Figure 10.1 The Transformative Power of Stories

Storytellers Are Made, Not Born

You may be reading this chapter thinking of some of the inspirational leaders who are great storytellers. If so, you're probably thinking: "I'll never be Martin Luther King. Storytelling is a gift and a mystery." Not so, I say from experience. It's something I've struggled with and learned to practice. In my case, practice hasn't made perfect, but it has made me much better.

Everyone has a story, and the act of figuring yours out will help you become more precise about why it is you care about an issue. Teachers often default to their students' stories. Those have a time and place, but so does your own.

One resource I've found helpful is the work of Andy Goodman. The following is his list of what he calls the ten immutable laws of storytelling.[5]

The Ten Immutable Laws of Storytelling

1. Stories are about people. (Name names)
2. The people in your story have to want something. (Goal)
3. Stories need to be fixed in time and space. (Setting)
4. Let your characters speak for themselves. (Voice)
5. Audiences bore easily. (Keep it snappy)
6. Stories speak the audience's language. (No jargon)
7. Stories stir up emotions. (Go for the laugh, the cry, the heartstrings)
8. Stories don't tell: they show.

9. Stories have at least one "moment of truth."

10. Stories have clear meaning.

I have actually used this as a checklist to review my own speeches and writing. Good storytelling looks effortless. Behind the scenes, it involves mundane tasks like thinking through how the puzzle pieces of a story fit together, figuring out where to add detail and where to subtract it, and driving home a moral point (that perhaps gets repeated during the telling).

Common pitfalls I've seen among beginning storytellers include being too generic, trying to tell one's whole life story, and trying to make too many points at once. All of these are easy to fix if you treat your oral story the way you would an essay. Try a rough draft and then edit accordingly.

Storytellers have the power to ignite change, and storytelling is the first step in transforming your issue into a movement that inspires others to join you. With the knowledge you have gained in this book, I hope you will take that first step. Then buckle up: you're in for an unpredictable (but purposeful) ride.

Moving into Your Own Advocacy

The education sector is ever changing, and it is perhaps changing more rapidly than in the past. We will always have changing players in political seats; we will always have transitions. In the current era, we have a new presidential administration. Change is certainly coming to our schools. The choices teachers make about when and how to engage in the decisions that affect their classrooms will be huge determinants of whether their power grows or shrinks in the coming years.

I hope this book empowers you to take action and offers the tools needed to be successful in advocacy. I hope it provides a framework for understanding who is on the other side of the decision-making table and what that person is likely to be thinking and to be constrained by. I look forward to locking arms with you in the struggle to create schools where all of our kids can thrive and find happiness!

Key Takeaways

☐ Effective advocates connect their story of self to the story of the collective movement (story of us) and to the right moment (story of now).

☐ Major changes in education are often spurred by a larger galvanizing moment.

☐ Successful advocates find entry points for advancing their issue in the broader social context.

☐ Compelling advocacy stories have a challenge, a choice, and an outcome.

☐ Storytellers are made, not born.

Notes

1. Marshall Ganz, "Telling Your Public Story: Self, Us, Now" (2006), http://www
   .rmnetwork.org/newrmn/wp-content/BIC_Toolkit/Toolkit/story_content/
   external_files/Appendix_7_Telling_Your_Public_Story.pdf, 38.
2. Douglas N. Harris, "Good News for New Orleans,"
   EducationNext 15, no. 4 (Fall 2015), http://educationnext.org/
   good-news-new-orleans-evidence-reform-student-achievement/.
3. Stephen Brill, *Class Warfare: Inside the Fight to Fix America's Schools* (New
   York: Simon & Schuster, 2011), 227.
4. Ganz, "Telling Your Public Story," 37.
5. Andy Goodman, "The Ten Immutable Laws of Storytelling," Visual
   Story Network (n.d.), http://www.visualstorynetwork.org/page/
   the-10-immutable-laws-of-storytelling.

INDEX

Page references followed by *fig* indicate an illustrated figure; followed by *t* indicate a table.

CPSIA information can be obtained
at www.ICGtesting.com
Printed in the USA
JSHW012040300623
43985JS00003B/176